MW00416070

A Shield Against the Monster
Copyright © 2019 Carol Hart Metzker and Ann Marie Jones

Printed in the United States of America

Cover Design: Melissa K. Thomas

Copy Editing: Lori Stephens

Luminare Press
442 Charnelton
Eugene, OR 97401
www.luminarepress.com

LCCN: 2019910836
ISBN: 978-1-64388-191-1

Protecting Children from Human Trafficking

A SHIELD AGAINST THE
MONSTER

Carol Hart Metzker and Ann Marie Jones

LUMINARE PRESS

WWW.LUMINAREPRESS.COM

To my parents, who gave me roots and wings,
as the saying goes, and a loving home to grow
them, and to my daughters, who are now gracing
the world with their own roots and wings.

—C. H. M.

To my three beautiful daughters that they may
live happy, joyous, and free, and also to Dawn's
Place for giving me my life back. I thought
it was lost, but now it is found.

—A. M. J.

Contents

Part 1

THE FACE OF THE MONSTER

Part 2

PLAYBOOK

Please Don't Skip
This Preface

Carol

WHEN I LOOKED INTO THE EYES OF MY NEWBORN daughters, Elizabeth in 1989 and Kathryn in 1992, I saw the depths and magnificence of the universe. I wanted profound love, safety, and the world's most wonderful experiences for my children.

I also experienced fear—sometimes real, sometimes irrational—that something bad would happen to them. The list of things that could hurt them was all too vast. At that time, I didn't even consider something that parents today face: the monster of human trafficking. It was there but in disguise and so rarely discussed that I didn't know it existed.

When my younger daughter was eleven, I met an eleven-year-old girl in India who had been enslaved in the circus and sold for sex. Before that encounter, human trafficking—referred to as modern slavery in countries outside of the United States—existed for me as a horrible relic of the past or a sensationalized Hollywood plot. What if she were mine? Feeling devastated by that experience, I set out to help fight the monster of human trafficking and to lend a hand to organizations helping survivors.

For more than a decade, I've worked on projects for victims and survivors and toward the prevention of additional victims of violence, drug abuse, and harm that often accompanies trafficking. I've volunteered with survivors of human trafficking and commercial sexual exploitation (CSE) and consulted with The Salvation Army's New Day to Stop Trafficking Program. My book, *Facing the Monster: How One Person Can Fight Child Slavery* (Open Books, 2012), was penned to show how ordinary people can help disable the system of human trafficking without being a saint, millionaire, or world traveler.

Hundreds of speeches, delivered close to my home in Pennsylvania and as far away as Sydney and Seoul, have encouraged people from all walks of life to take action. I have made some presentations with Ann Marie Jones, an extraordinary woman and survivor with whom I volunteered years ago. Over time, my educational programs have focused increasingly on sex trafficking and CSE in the United States.

Questions arise from every audience. Early on, the most common questions were as follows:

- **Human trafficking doesn't happen *here*, does it?** Yes, no matter where *here* is.

- **Isn't prostitution a choice?** Although some people tell me that they know someone who says she or he wants that lifestyle, neither Ann Marie nor I have met anyone who tells us so. No four-year-old girl has such aspirations, and no young people look for a table at a career fair because they're hoping for such a life. Survivors tell us the opposite: they ended up in such a position because of force, fraud, or coercion, or because they believed there was nothing else available to them for food, money, diapers for their children, or survival. Some told me that when they were on the street, they defended their right to do as they pleased with their bodies because it was better to believe they had control over their lives than to believe that they were hopelessly controlled by someone else. Psychological chains are every bit as effective, yet damaging, as physical ones.

- **Don't girls sell themselves just to pay for drugs?** From talking to survivors including Ann Marie, I've learned that substance abuse or addiction stems from numbing pain. Sometimes victims use drugs or alcohol to relieve pain that comes from childhood abuse. Traffickers, or pimps, sometimes exploit women through their previous addiction. In other cases, traffickers introduce drugs and facilitate addiction as a method of control. Only recently has the judicial system begun to operate from the perspective that it is illegal to exploit humans by using their addiction against them—the same way it is illegal to sexually take advantage of a person or to have anyone sign a contract or document when they are not lucid and able to give consent.

Today the monster of human trafficking is front and center, waiting to see who is fighting back and who isn't. Today a common question I hear is this: **How do I protect my child from human trafficking?**

In this book, Ann Marie and I shine a light on answers to that question.

Ann Marie

When my first daughter, Linda, was born, I saw the most beautiful child in the world. I was going to be the best mother to this child. I had hopes and dreams for her to be successful in life because I would raise her with respect and morals. I wanted to protect her, keep her safe.

She was molested at the age of thirteen by my younger brother. It hit me like a ton of bricks because another one of my brothers had molested me at that age. When I realized that I couldn't protect her, I felt worthless and ashamed. I felt like I wasn't a good mother. It sent my life and Linda's into a downward spiral.

As readers will learn, my life took a detour.

More than ten years later when I became pregnant with my twin daughters, I was filled with fear. I was homeless, on drugs, and in the streets being prostituted and controlled by a monster—a man who told me after we were involved in a relationship that he was a pimp from New York. Newly pregnant, I thought that I had a chance to do parenthood over again, to be a good mother, and to keep my children safe even though I was living in a world of chaos and confusion.

I made the decision to get away from the street and the man who controlled me. I checked into a rehab center that allowed children to stay with their moms. I stayed there until the babies were four months old. After my twins were born, I took parenting classes and learned how to be a better mother. I had hopes and dreams of living in a house with a white picket fence, with the sun shining on me and my children…living within normal society.

After another detour during which I lost everything precious, some special recovery and rehabilitation programs helped me retake control of my life. Today, Linda and I have reunited, and I have regained custody of my twins. I work as a peer counselor at Dawn's Place, a residence for female survivors, where I learned to heal and got help. It's also where I met my coauthor, Carol Metzker. My criminal record has been expunged. I tell my story at churches, anti-human trafficking conferences, and Narcotics Anonymous conventions. Carol and I have bumped into each other in Harrisburg, our state capitol, while advocating for better laws against human trafficking.

Sometimes it's difficult to tell my story. It's hard when I talk about my children and when I talk about being molested as a child. It's hard remembering when I was told to sweep it under the rug and when no one helped. It's hard when I feel like I failed or like I'm being blamed for something out of my control.

I want this book to let people know that human trafficking is a reality. It doesn't happen only on TV. Once I walked into the store to buy plants and told the shopkeeper they were for a residence for women involved in human trafficking and CSE. "It really happens here?" she said.

If I can help just one person open their eyes to the truth of sex trafficking and keep a child from being sold, opening myself and sharing my story will be worth it.

Together We Are Better

Both of us, Carol and Ann Marie, are moms with daughters. We come from families with different backgrounds, have different life experiences, and have needed to adapt to different and ever-changing environments for rearing children, yet we share similar philosophies of parenting. We hold the same dreams of happiness and safety for our daughters and the world's children.

We believe that by sharing our knowledge and experiences—some negative and some positive—we can help beat back the monster of human trafficking. We believe that if parents, teachers, coaches, caregivers, and neighbors practice and adapt the tips we provide in this book, fewer of our fellow humans will endure the devastating pain of a crime that should not—and must not—happen ever again.

Please Don't Skip This Introduction Either

WHILE WORKING ON THIS BOOK, CAROL FOUND ON A Facebook page explicit instructions for pimps—human traffickers—to break a female in order to control her and sell her for sex.

> *You need to get that b*tch to do sh*t she don't want to do. This can really be anything but it's better if it's sexual…The reason for this is you need to break her and show her your new control over her (asterisks added by coauthors).[1]*

Tactics described were violent, sexual, degrading, and shocking. In short, they were atrocious.

Pimps—human traffickers—have playbooks and instructional videos for recruiting and selling kids for sex.

This book gives people who care about kids a playbook for fighting back. It is designed to provide practical information to help protect your children and others in the community from the harm that comes from human trafficking and modern slavery. It focuses on sex trafficking and CSE because of our work experience with survivors and Ann Marie's experience as a survivor. The action items, however, can also help protect kids against other harm: sexual abuse, turning to drugs to numb pain and feelings of isolation, cyberbullying, and other traumatic experiences. We include numerous stories about the people and situations we have encountered, but unless we have their permission or they have spoken publicly, we do not share real names for their privacy and anonymity. Names that are changed are marked with an asterisk.

For the reader's ease, we (Carol and Ann Marie) use "I" or "we" in the stories throughout the book. In many instances, we use the terms "they" and "their" instead of "he or she" and "his or her" for brevity and respect for people within a full range of gender identities who need protection from the monster of human trafficking.

The book is divided into four sections: the first with enough background information to get you started and then twenty-five action items to build a shield.

1. The Face of the Monster: Basic information to introduce readers to human trafficking: where it is, what it is, what it means to be a victim, what makes a child vulnerable to trafficking, and why it's so important to shield children from this crime.

2. What You Can Do: Enhance Parenting/Mentoring Skills—Eight tips and action items for creating a better *you* as a parent or person in the community who works with or cares about kids.

3. What You Can Do: Strengthen Children— Eight tips and action items for strengthening your children.

4. What You Can Do: Build a Safer Community—Nine tips and action items for building a community where traffickers and trafficking cannot flourish.

In the sections about what you can do, each tip or action item has its own chapter. Throughout the book, boxes with statistics to further illuminate the issue or additional resources are provided.

Read or use the book in the way that makes sense to you, starting on page 1 and finishing on the last page, or start with action items in the section that interests you most, and refer to basic information about human trafficking when you need it. The book is designed for busy people (and aren't we all?) to take one short chapter/action at a time. Practice an action that you can work into your daily life. Move onto another chapter or learn another tip when you're ready and have another moment. Take action.

Terms Used in This Book

The following terms are listed in order of what you need to know and then to build on your knowledge, not in alphabetical order.

Human trafficking: A form of modern slavery, making someone commit a sex or labor act against their will through force, fraud, or coercion. Note: A person doesn't have to be moved from one place to another to be a victim.

Sex trafficking: Selling someone or making them commit a sex act through force, fraud, or coercion unless the victim is younger than eighteen. If a child is being sold for sex, it is sex trafficking whether or not force, fraud, or coercion is involved.

Commercial sexual exploitation (CSE): The exchange of money, goods, or services for sex; being sold for sex.

Commercial sexual exploitation of children (CSEC): Can involve selling a child for sex or pornography.

In the life: Involved in CSE.

Pimp: Person who sells or drums up sales for sex. Note: A victim probably will not call a pimp a pimp but will call a male "daddy" or refer to him as a boyfriend.

John/Trick/Date: A person who buys sex; called a "punter" in many countries outside of the United States.

Victim: Someone still being sold for sex. Sometimes the term is used for a person who was sold for sex in the past instead of using the term "survivor."

Survivor: Someone who was formerly sold for sex or held in labor trafficking.

Why We Don't Like the Words Prostitution or Prostitute

Few people choose to sell their bodies as a career. Some are prostituted through force, fraud, or coercion. Others believe there is no other option for earning the money they need for survival or getting out of a situation they haven't chosen. Although some people are lured into trying it and the fantasy that it will be a life they control, filled with glamour and money in a short period of time, victims find that the fantasy was false. Commercial sexual exploitation robs victims of freedom, safety, money, health, dignity, and—all too often—life itself.

We also do not use the term "sex worker." Paraphrasing a group of survivors who have experienced torture, degradation by consumers, and loss of control over their lives, the notion that sex work is empowerment rather than violence is BS.[2]

Part 1

THE FACE OF
THE MONSTER

CHAPTER 1

You Want Me to Do *What?*

THE AVERAGE AGE OF FORMAL ENTRY INTO COMMER-cial sexual exploitation, what many people erroneously call child prostitution, in the United States is eleven to fourteen.[3] Putting it in a different way, in the United States, the heinous monster of human trafficking strikes kids at the age of eleven to fourteen when they're practicing multiplication tables or learning algebra, reading elementary mysteries, or playing middle school soccer.

That's the *average* age. In some countries, it's even younger. What could be more shocking and horrifying?

No one thinks they will be the next victim. No little kid aspires to be sold for sex. No one deserves it, yet it happens. Tragically, the injustice is widespread. Astonishingly, some people believe that it doesn't happen in their community. Over the past eleven years, the Federal Bureau of Investigation Operation Cross Country efforts alone have recovered nearly one thousand child victims.[4]

At eleven to fourteen years old, children can't consent to sex, so how they be child prostitutes? The answer is they can't. They are victims of human trafficking and sex trafficking, a form of modern slavery.

Consider this too. A child may be sold for sex or groomed for such a life from six years old to 17 years and 364 days. They may know no other existence. On their eighteenth birthday, if caught by law enforcement in some states, they can be arrested and imprisoned as a criminal prostitute if unable to prove force, fraud, or coercion into what is called "the life." In other situations, childhood experiences make adults vulnerable to being sold for sex.

They probably will not identify as victims. They might claim that they—not a pimp, trafficker, boyfriend, partner, family member, or friend—are in control of their thoughts and actions. As coauthor Ann Marie said of her pimp/trafficker's past control of her, "When he says the sky is purple, you believe him. You know it's blue, but you believe it's purple."

Other survivors said when they insisted they controlled their own lives, "It was the drugs talking"—an addiction that an exploiter used against them. Others said they wanted so badly to believe that they were in control of something that they swore to anyone who would listen that they chose their actions, only to admit to themselves during recovery that they had lost every ounce of freedom and dignity.

Would you know the face of this monster if you saw it? Could you confront it? Could you help prevent it from preying on children in your home and community?

Eyes Wide Open

- 12 years: The average age of formal entry into CSE in the United States, Canada, and Mexico (Estes and Weiner, "The Commercial Sexual Exploitation of Children in the U.S., Canada and Mexico" 2001).[5]

- 7 years: Average life expectancy after someone has entered a life of CSE (Fang, "Young Lives for Sale" 2005).[6]

- $99 billion: Estimated total annual profits made from forced sexual exploitation...not including profits made on pornography of women and children against their will ("Profits and Poverty," International Labour Organization 2014).[7]

- 1 in 7 endangered runaways reported to the National Center for Missing & Exploited Children (NCMEC) in 2018 were likely sex trafficking victims (NCMEC 2019).[8]

- 20 percent of interviewed homeless youth were victims of some form of human trafficking (University of Pennsylvania 2018).[9]

- 24 percent of homeless lesbian, gay, bisexual, transgender, and queer or questioning (LGBTQ+) youth were trafficked for sex (Loyola University 2016).[10]

- Conservatively, more than 73 percent of child sex trafficking survivors say they lacked love or had a bad family situation (Thorn 2015).[11]

- 63 percent of child sex trafficking survivors were advertised online at some point during their trafficking situation (Thorn 2015).[12]

- 65 percent of victims of CSE of children deal with post-traumatic stress disorder (PTSD) (Farley et al. 2003).[13]

CHAPTER 2

A Victim, Not a Criminal

KAYLEY* HAD HAD ENOUGH. AT FOURTEEN YEARS OLD, she was tired of arguing with her parents, struggling at school, and wishing she was a popular girl with a boyfriend. She felt lonely, isolated, and empty, so when a boy began to flirt with her through a new app on her phone, she responded. The two exchanged cellphone numbers and agreed to meet at a nearby hangout.

He was older, cute, and attentive. In a single conversation, Kayley poured out her troubles to him. He responded. He told her she was pretty and that she deserved better treatment from everyone. He asked if she'd like to go out on a real date. With a smile, she got into his car.

No abduction. Nothing that seemed out of the ordinary. No one noticing that anything was wrong.

He offered her a cool new purse, promises of love, and a happy future. Then he turned on her. He threatened her life and sold her for sex.

By the time Kayley was seventeen, she had lived in an abandoned building, been forced to post nude photos of herself in online ads, experienced food being withheld as a means of controlling her, been choked to make sure she wasn't hiding money within her body, and become addicted to drugs to numb the pain of being raped by multiple men every day. She had been arrested for prostitution and was shunned and derided as "trash" by passersby. She assumed she was inherently bad and blamed herself. She trusted no one.

Kayley was a victim of human trafficking. She didn't know it. People who saw her didn't know it, and the men who paid to have sex with her didn't bother to question it.

She survived through street smarts, resilience, strength, and courage for years until law enforcement officers found her during a brothel raid. The officers listened to a victim advocate who recognized her as a child and victim who needed help.

Kayley's story is shared by far too many children and adults. The details vary—the situation that makes a victim vulnerable including socioeconomic status, strife or dysfunction within the home, low self-esteem, gender and background of the trafficker or pimp, methods of manipulation or force, type of exploitation, and other factors. The endurance of hell and life-altering trauma is consistent.

CHAPTER 3

Human Trafficking 101

After Carol had volunteered with survivors and worked on projects for a few years, she began enlisting the help of the community by giving educational speeches. She started by addressing small groups near her Pennsylvania home and by talking about projects for local survivors. Often a member of the audience asked a question afterward.

"Carol, when you say human trafficking is here, you don't really mean it is here, do you? We know it's a problem in India, Africa, and former Soviet states, but you didn't mean it's here in southeastern Pennsylvania, did you?" The question was repeated by audiences and individuals in ten states. Each time she replied, "Yes, it's here."

In 2014, Carol visited Nepal with two other Rotarians to check on some projects they had undertaken to help survivors of sex slavery in Kathmandu. While there, they spoke to a group of businessmen about their work. As an audience member drove them to their guesthouse, he asked, "Carol, when you say sex slavery is a problem here, you don't mean it's here, do you? We know it's a problem in the West and the United States, but you didn't really mean in Kathmandu, did you?"

Carol received the same question thousands of miles and a couple of years apart. *You don't really mean it's here, do you?*

As the question was the same, the answer was the same. Yes, it is here, no matter where *here* is, but unless human trafficking has affected us in a personal way that we know about, it seems nearly impossible to believe that it is a problem in the beautiful place we call home. As a society, we must overcome disbelief and denial to stop this injustice.

An estimated 3.8 million adults worldwide were victims of forced sexual exploitation and one million children were victims of sexual exploitation in 2016. Most victims—99 percent—were women and girls.[14]

What It Is

Although some state and federal definitions of human trafficking can differ slightly, they are similar to this one in the US Code/Trafficking Victims Protection Act:

Sex trafficking is the recruitment, harboring, transportation, provision, obtaining, patronizing, or soliciting of a person for the purposes of a commercial sex act, in which the commercial sex act is induced by force, fraud, or coercion, or in which the person induced to perform such an act has not attained 18 years of age (22 USC § 7102).

Labor trafficking is the recruitment, harboring, transportation, provision, or obtaining of a person for labor or services, through the use of force, fraud, or coercion for the purposes of subjection to involuntary servitude, peonage, debt bondage, or slavery (22 USC § 7102).

There are different forms of human trafficking: labor and sex, forced child marriage, child soldiering, debt bondage, organ harvesting, and others. People do not have to be transported or moved to be victims. Sometimes they endure more than one form during physical or psychological captivity. All forms are devastating to the human body and spirit.

Human trafficking is modern slavery. For most readers, the terms and definitions don't adequately convey the meaning of the crime in such a way that they comprehend the victims' reality. What does it really mean to be a victim of sex trafficking?

CHAPTER 4

What It Means to Be a Victim of Sex Trafficking

ANN MARIE DESCRIBED THE LIFE OF TRAFFICKED KIDS she saw while living with her own devastation. "They were experiencing chaos. Loneliness. Unhappiness. Shame. Grief over losing themselves. Fear. There were a lot of things to be afraid of—getting into a car and never coming back, weapons, afraid of being beaten by pimps or johns, or that no one would ever care for them. They were even afraid of themselves." Victims of sex trafficking experience the following:

- Betrayal

- Unsafe living conditions

- Extreme violence

- Psychological bondage

- Sex ten to fifteen times each day on average (Shared Hope International)

- Isolation and shunning by society

Betrayal

Betrayal comes from traffickers who profess love and from the institutions most people in society hold dear: members , of family, law enforcement/the judicial system, and faith-based organizations.

Traffickers can be any gender, and they are informally categorized in different ways: guerilla pimps (those who use violence), sneaker pimps (teens or young people who "casually" sell girls on the school playground or from their neighborhood or community circles at the other end of the spectrum from organized crime rings or gangs), Romeo pimps, and others.

A Romeo pimp preys on a girl who longs for love, acceptance, and a better home life. He seeks girls who are vulnerable because of sexual or physical abuse, home-lessness, low self-esteem, poverty, youth and naiveté, learning differences, neglect, family strife, or instability. Online or in person, he promises love and a romantic future. Promises dissolve when she is threatened, forced, deceived, cajoled, or coerced by him into stripping at a bachelor party, posing for pornography, having sex with his friends, and ultimately being sold for sex. Despite being sold for sex, living with violence, or being in a situation where multiple women are held by the same man, a victim hangs onto the thought that her "boyfriend," as she calls him, loves her.

Betrayal by institutions that are supposed to protect children happens when they are the problem instead of the protector. Examples include the following:

- A family member "grooms"—gains trust and then abuses it or creates a situation in which a child doesn't grasp that harm is abnormal and illegal—and then sells a child for sex.

- A leader, employee, or member of a church, synagogue, mosque, or other house of worship sells a girl or a member of that organization is a "john"—consumer of sex—who pays to rape her (even if he believes he is "just having sex," if she cannot consent, it is rape).

- A law enforcement officer says he will arrest her for prostitution unless she has sex with him (sometimes it happens, and she is arrested anyway) or a law enforcement officer or court official pays to have sex with a victim.

Betrayal is complete when society doesn't believe or blames the victim because the betrayer is popular, powerful, and in a position to be believed. Community leaders can be the last to be suspected because of their history of doing well or doing good in the community.

Dr. Marlene Carson is a survivor of child sex trafficking who survived to found Rahab's Hideaway residential treatment facility and develop an antihuman trafficking network called Switch. Years ago, a charismatic couple from her church arranged a trip to New York City for a group of teen girls from their congregation, including Marlene. In New York, the couple gave the girls sexy clothing and told them not to come back to their hotel until they had reached a quota of money. After the group's return home—without one of the girls—the husband helped lead false efforts to find the missing minor. His wife continued the charade as far as feeding Marlene soup when the girl withdrew from community life as a result of trauma. Admiration, not suspicion, was heaped upon the couple.[15]

Unsafe Living Conditions

Victims live in unsafe, unhealthy conditions. Sometimes the conditions are squalid.

Ann Marie called the abandoned building where she once lived her "abandominium." The term implying posh surroundings, and revealing her sense of humor, made the building without heat, lights, hot water, and working toilets seem more tolerable. Other survivors talk about making futile attempts to clean around crumbling walls or to fall asleep while hearing the scratch of rodents.

Some victims don't have "abandominiums"—they collapse in alleys or near train tracks. While on the street, Ann Marie knew an older woman who exploited her seventeen-year-old daughter. They slept in a park. "When winter got really cold, a trick would sometimes let me stay at his house and eat and shower," Ann Marie recounted. "Even though I was on the street, doing drugs, doing the same thing she was doing, I'd take the girl a bowl of food from his house and try to get her off the street."

Other unhealthy living conditions are invisible to outsiders. In a small town near Carol's, a mother advertised her preteen daughter online as she looked for money to pay for her drug habit. No one was the wiser until a community member discovered a video on social media. (Authorities and social agencies were properly alerted; the child is now safe.) Some young victims have lived in homes and attended school in unsuspecting suburban neighborhoods while being sold for sex under the control of a gang. Too many victims are being sold within a home where domestic violence and psychological abuse overlap with sex trafficking.

Violence

Neither Carol as a volunteer nor Ann Marie as a peer counselor has worked with a survivor who didn't experience violence. The violence was weekly if not daily or many times in a day. Secondary or reflective trauma—watching, hearing, or listening to the story of brutal beatings or rapes against other victims—compounded mental and emotional damage.

One of the most psychologically damaging aspects of the violence is not knowing when it will happen next or who will inflict it. Ann Marie said that having to be aware of potential violence every minute of the day had nearly the same effect as exposure to actual violence every waking moment.

The violence is horrific—being beaten, harmed with weapons or household tools used as weapons, raped, and sometimes tortured by pimps/traffickers or johns. At The Salvation Army's New Day Women's Drop-in Center for victims experiencing sex trafficking and CSE, staff and volunteers report that the most common medical problem they see is wounds.

Sometimes violence toward women is so severe it results in death. In 2016, women "in the life" in Philadelphia were targeted by a serial killer with a machete. Although there was a video recording of the man believed to be responsible for three murders in three months, to date the killer has not been caught.

Consequently, approximately two-thirds of victims end up with PTSD. Episodes can include flashbacks, nightmares, disturbing thoughts, strong reactions to sounds, sights, or smells that "trigger" responses to the original trauma, and more. The intensity of episodes experienced by victims of human trafficking can be as severe as that experienced by combat victims.[16]

Brendale McAfee, a survivor who is now a staff member at Dawn's Place, a residential program for female survivors, said, "To hear all our stories, we'd be swimming in tears."

Sex Ten to Fifteen Times/Day on Average

On average, US victims have sex ten to fifteen times per day every single day of the year for as long as they are in psychological or physical bondage. Sex is often with strangers and victims are exposed to pain, violence, unwanted pregnancy, skin conditions, and illnesses that range from the common cold to sexually transmitted infections including HIV/AIDS.

While in India, Carol met a seven-year-old girl who was rescued the first day she was sold. She was so distraught that a man who had paid to rape her telephoned her sister but not before she had been violated by multiple johns.

Trauma/Psychological Bonding

Although people sometimes have a mental image of a victim

in shackles or chains, and some victims are held in physical captivity, most victims today are held in another insidious way: trauma bonding or psychological bonding. Over time or through a series of a trafficker's deliberate actions, a victim may come to feel love, affection, or trust toward the person who is inflicting harm.

When a trafficker deliberately sets up mixed messages that instill both fear of death and gratitude for being allowed to live, victims end up with complex, confused emotions and physical reactions.[17] The resulting scrambled feelings from brain trauma are why victims don't seek help and don't identify themselves as victims. Often, they defend or side with the trafficker and refuse to testify against a trafficker because of a combination of death threats and the belief that true love is just around the corner.

One example of a method of trauma bonding is withholding of food for a long period of time until a quota of money is given to the trafficker. (More than a few of us would struggle to earn $1,500 in order to eat our next meal in a day!) Many hours later, when the victim returns with the quota, feelings of starvation, anxiety, and emotional upheaval have set in. As food is presented, the victim experiences a positive mental and physical response—euphoria and gratitude—directed toward the provider of the food. While the trafficker is responsible for withholding food, the more immediate feeling of the trafficker as hero for solving the problem overshadows earlier negative feelings.

Like many victims of sex trafficking, Jessica had a baby with her trafficker. The pimp threatened to rape their preschool daughter unless she brought back enough money to suit him. Fear of him harming their child, her belief that he was providing food and shelter for the baby in a way that she couldn't, and numerous other complex emotions kept Jessica tied to the man who kept her life in shambles.

Isolation and Shunning by Society

Despite having to endure such horrors, females are often viewed as criminals, not victims, as bad girls who choose or want to sell themselves to support a drug habit. They are shunned by "nicer" members of society, sometimes by the same individuals who at other times pay to have sex with them. They end up as the butt of jokes, are called nasty names, and are viewed and treated as trash. They are seen as objects or roles rather than as humans.

A nun who reaches out to victims in a red-light district of Philadelphia once asked a young woman on a street corner how she was feeling. The young woman was shocked. She said that staff at a medical clinic she sometimes visited asked if she had any sexually transmitted infections, but no one had ever asked how she felt in general or checked her cholesterol.

After being raped on the street, Ann Marie reported the crime to the police. Two officers drove her around the area to look for the rapist. Unable to find him, they stopped, and the police got out. Sitting in the back seat of the patrol car with the window rolled down, she overheard one officer say to another, "What's the difference? She's just a whore." She felt like she had been violated again.

Instead of being treated with compassion, victims of CSE are often marginalized and blamed for their own circumstances.

Short Lived

Is it any wonder then that the average life expectancy of a victim, after entering CSE, is seven years?[18]

Marian Hatcher—a survivor who does groundbreaking work in the Cook County Sherriff's Office in Illinois and coordinates stings to stop johns—helps shatter myths about the sex trade. Many people think that glamour and big money are found in the life, she says, but those who end up there find out that more likely, and far too quickly, life will end in a coffin.

The stories of far too many victims of sex trafficking, known and unknown by Carol and Ann Marie, speak of tragedy. Anna died of a drug overdose when trying to cope with all that had happened to her as a child and young adult; she was twenty-six years old when Carol and Ann Marie attended her funeral. Jessica's heart gave out before her youngest child entered kindergarten.

Lack of healthcare and exposure to countless diseases, drug overdose from numbing, and suicide from depression and hopelessness end the lives of victims and survivors. What if we began to recognize what makes a child vulnerable to trafficking before it happens?

CHAPTER 5

Vulnerability

ANYTHING THAT SEEMS TO MAKE SOMEONE LESS interesting to mainstream society makes him or her valuable to a trafficker. Anytime people don't have options for fulfilling needs or longings, they become vulnerable to trafficking. Vulnerabilities include the following:

- Feeling unloved

- Low self-esteem

- Domestic violence, sexual abuse, or strife in the home

- Learning differences or illiteracy

- LGBTQ+ and other gender-based oppression or rejection

- Race

- Homelessness or poverty

- Alcohol or drug abuse

- Depression or other mental health issues

- Loneliness, isolation, or lack of belonging

- Lack of options or perceived lack of options

- Any factors that leave a child in the welfare system

What might look like a happy home from the outside might be a place where there is physical or psychological abuse or neglect behind closed doors. A well-to-do, beautiful young woman who had been a straight-A student and sports team captain ran from a home where her parents demanded perfection in every aspect. She was sold for sex. Rebecca Bender, another sex trafficking survivor and now founder of an organization that trains first responders and service providers who help victims, was afraid to tell her parents that she was pregnant as a teen. The man she turned to for help sold her for sex.

A trafficker draws out a child's voids, fears, or longings and quickly fills those gaps or reassures the fears to build a false trusting relationship. A girl who wants a boyfriend is provided romance and gifts that symbolize love. Youth who are homeless because of rejection by family and society are promised food and shelter. Promises dissolve quickly, kids are sold for sex, and their trust is used against them.

Ann Marie's vulnerabilities were exploited as an adult, but they stemmed from childhood experiences as her story shows.

CHAPTER 6

Ann Marie's Story:
Out of the Black Hole

ANN MARIE DREAMED OF LIVING IN A HOUSE SUR-rounded by a picket fence and filled with love for as long as she could remember having a dream.

In reality, her home life was chaos. Her single mother, an alcoholic, was raising several children on a waitress's wages. Most of the time, she was working or drinking at a bar. Ann Marie's alcoholic, abusive father left when she was three. Her older sister functioned as a parent—cooking dinner, hiding the younger siblings when her father sometimes showed up drunk, and visiting the school principal to have Ann Marie reinstated after being suspended.

One night when Ann Marie was thirteen, she woke up as her brother was molesting her. Terrified, she didn't move until he fell asleep. She ran to tell her mother. Instead of being comforted and taken for professional help, she was slapped and instructed not to tell anyone, as her brother slept on without consequence.

Hard-pressed to prove anyone cared, Ann Marie began to refer to herself as "No Name." She tested limits. By the time she was seventeen, she was running away from home and looking for attention from boys. Untreated trauma further complicated school challenges caused by language processing and learning differences. She began to skip school. After a while, she skipped so often that no one realized she was gone.

At eighteen, she became pregnant, got married, and worked hard to start a happy, "white picket fence" home. Unconsciously she repressed memories of being molested, and for a decade, life was better with her husband and daughter, Linda.

Ann Marie was at work when she got the call that Linda, thirteen years old, had been molested by Ann Marie's younger brother. The dam holding back memories of her own molestation broke, flooding her with old pain on top of new. Her sister turned against Ann Marie when she revealed and fought back against her brother's crime on behalf of her daughter. Unable to bear the agony, her husband began to drink. She found that drugs numbed everything. Without tools to stop the downward spiral, she turned to the solution that had worked somewhat when she was thirteen. She left home.

She was homeless, using drugs, and trying to survive more chaos and anguish than ever. Without knowing anything about the streets, she began the life (what society calls prostitution) under the "El"—the elevated train tracks in Philly. She felt dirty. Disgusting. Disgraced. She got the first of many new names: A.M.

After being beaten one night on the street, a man said he would rescue her and love her the way she deserved. Instead of ending up in a relationship in a house with a picket fence, she ended up in an abandoned building. She found out that the man was a pimp from New York City who had a house in Pennsylvania. He took her five-gallon buckets of cold water to use for bathing at the abandoned building, sent her onto the streets to earn money for him, and asked her to work in Atlantic City, New Jersey, where casinos attracted patrons with money. She still called him her boyfriend and believed that one day he would treat her better. When she told him she was pregnant with his twins, he backhanded her across the face.

With the help of hospital nurses, she checked herself into a safe home for women and their children and stayed until her baby daughters were four months old. She remained "clean" (not using drugs) and received healthcare and counseling. Although her pimp paid other women to find her, she stayed away from him. Unfortunately, he and his false promises to treat her right were at the door the day she left the home. Believing she had a second chance to create a happy, loving life for her children, she went with him.

Deceived again, she ended up at his house where he lived with another woman as his wife. He presented the babies to his "wife," who took the twins away from Ann Marie and relegated her to the sofa. He beat Ann Marie as he had done before. In less than a year, her dreams of a beautiful new life had crumbled. She ran back to life on the streets and drugs to take away the larger-than-before grief and mental torture.

During the years she spent in the life, she was raped and beaten by johns and her pimp. Without questioning whether she was a victim or criminal, she was arrested and convicted for prostitution more than ten times, yet in no cases were the johns arrested. She wanted out of her situation so badly that one day she tried to kill herself behind an abandoned house.

Years later, she described that period as living in a black hole. She could see the light at the top, but every time she climbed higher to get there, she fell back in, deeper than ever. She tried to quit the drugs, but with no place to go and no one to help, there were no options for making a change. The only way she had figured out to stop was by going to jail, another place where she found sexual exploitation, deprivation, and violence. The final time she was arrested for prostitution, she told the police "thank you." Jail wasn't the perfect way out, but it was a way.

From prison, she found a series of rehabilitation programs where she could heal. The day an officer transported her—while she wore shackles—to the first residential program, she told him he would never see her again. She was going to turn her life around. At Interim House and Dawn's Place, she received medical and psychological treatment to address years of layers of trauma. She took classes to learn the English and math skills she missed when she left school, eventually raising her reading level from third grade to college level. Through a special diversion court called Project Dawn Court, her criminal record was expunged. She used the strength, resilience, and determination that helped her survive the streets to build a new life.

Today she is a peer counselor at Dawn's Place, helping women exit and heal from the life she once endured. She and Linda have reunited, and she has custody of her twin daughters. Their home has a sunny kitchen with flowers in the windows and a small, outdoor deck with a wrought-iron fence.

What if someone had recognized Ann Marie's vulnerabilities as a teen? What if they had seen the indicators of sex trafficking and understood that she was a victim the first time she was exploited, arrested, or entered an emergency room?

We cannot change history, but we can create a new future. What would you be willing to do to prevent your child or another from enduring what Ann Marie did? If you could protect even one child, would you do it?

The next three sections provide specific, practical tips for taking action.

- Enhancing your parenting/mentoring skills

- Strengthening children

- Building a safer community

It will take work on all three levels. Even with help, children do not have mature reasoning, physical strength, experience, or power to fully protect themselves. You will need to build your own skills and improve the community. The whole village must take responsibility for the safety of all children.

Part 2

PLAYBOOK

What You Can Do: Enhance Parenting/Mentoring Skills

THERE IS ONLY ONE PERSON YOU CAN FULLY CHANGE: you. You can teach your children and work to improve your community. Ultimately, however, you cannot control the actions of kids, neighbors, or the larger community. Start taking action by enhancing your own parenting or mentoring skills.

Chances are you already care. You probably already do a million things right. Applaud those things (it's not easy being a parent—Carol and Ann Marie know!). Stretch them and enhance them. You know a lot—just add to that knowledge. Create a better *you*.

Action 1: Recognize the Monster's Profile

Take this quick quiz on what a trafficker looks like.

1. What sex is a trafficker?
   a. Male
   b. Female
   c. LGBTQ+
   d. All of the above

2. What age bracket is a trafficker?
   a. 15–20 years old
   b. 21–30 years old
   c. 31–45 years old
   d. 45 and older
   e. All of the above

3. What socioeconomic background does a trafficker have?
   a. Below the poverty line
   b. Middle-class
   c. Wealthy
   d. All of the above

4. What work clothes does a trafficker tend to wear?
   a. Jeans and sneakers
   b. Business suit
   c. Stylish dresses or pants with trendy accessories
   d. Athletic wear
   e. All of the above

5. Traffickers look like:
   a. A friend or family member
   b. Someone different from you
   c. All of the above

If you answered "All of the above" for every question, you were 100 percent correct. Traffickers come in all shapes, sizes, colors, gender identities, socioeconomic backgrounds, and walks of life. While we tend to think of them as charismatic or outgoing, they have different personalities. The ugly truth is that they can be quiet parents from wealthy backgrounds who sell their children inside their homes, gregarious high school students in jeans and sneakers who sell other students after class, businessmen in suits who conduct a side business from their full-time offices, gorgeous women who claim to have a girl's back at the mall after she has had a fight with her mom, and people who look similar to you, no matter what you look like.

They are identified by their behaviors: grooming and selling another human being for sex.

Once you know that a trafficker can look like anyone, you can be open to the possibility that a situation isn't necessarily what it seems on the surface. You can be more prepared to trust your instinct or someone else's words when they voice suspicions or a complaint. You can be ready to keep an eye open for signs of victimization: scars, brands, or signs of abuse; a teenage girl with an older boyfriend and fancy gifts; a changing story; signs of depression or substance abuse; or fear of authority figures (see Action 17 for a longer list).

Action 2: Listen Up!

Carol and Ann Marie conducted a workshop about protecting children against sex trafficking at a Quaker meetinghouse in the country. Ann Marie's eleven-year-old twins had been exploring the grounds and rushed in with the news that they found two bones. Relatively accustomed to the sight of deer bones or antlers that had been shed in the woods and fields, Carol and the other participants said they'd go out later to look at the bones with the girls.

To the surprise of many, local police arrived a few minutes later. They followed the girls, investigated the situation, looked at the bones, found other remains of a deer close by, and closed the case.

What was so important about this situation was that the twins had something important to say, and the detectives listened intently. They took the kids' information seriously without making assumptions and checked it out.

How many times do we half-listen or make assumptions that we know the answer before we engage in the situation? Do we dismiss what children say because their info seems preposterous because it is out of *our* norm? Here's how to listen better.

- Listen and believe. For some reason, it is hard for many people to believe a victim unless they've been through something similar. It's hard to conceive that a person of faith or a prominent, popular community leader would secretly harm a child, but it happens, and we need to believe when children tell us. You do not need to discern by yourself whether or not a child's testimony is real—ask experts to help. Pull in crime victim advocates or police. Let experts investigate.

- Reach out and ask more questions—not just of your kids but also of other people who are around them when you're not. Ask teachers, relatives, or other parents: What is my child's personality like in the classroom or social situations? What are their friends like? Are there any behaviors that don't make sense to you?

- Practice reflective listening. When someone tells you something, repeat it back to them in question or statement form.

Child: My mom went to the hospital last night.

Teacher: Your mom was at the hospital last night?

Child: Yes. Maybe she ate something she shouldn't.

Teacher: Oh my. She ate something bad?

Child: Yes...

Sometimes at this point, the child will scamper off to play. They might have simply wanted to get the news off their chest and be heard. Sometimes the conversation will go further. The teacher might discover that the child is still worried or that something more serious is going on and a different response is needed.

Reflective listening is extremely important during disagreements, because it can shift the tone and outcome of the situation. When people feel that their side of the story or opinions haven't been heard and taken seriously, conflict can escalate, and trust can erode. Reflective listening demonstrates that the listener has truly listened. It provides the speaker with a chance to hear their own words and to clarify, explain, or rethink something they have said. Even if a kid's statements are incorrect or in poor judgment, sincerely and calmly repeat what they said before opposing them. You might understand their point from a different perspective.

Cut back on your own activities if you don't have time to listen. Make yourself available when they are ready to talk about serious problems, because there might not be a second time. If you don't listen when your child reports that another student bit them in pre-kindergarten, your son might not bother to say anything in middle school when he is being bullied, or your high school daughter may be silent when she is receiving unwanted attention.

One more word about listening: Campaigns and media often depict victims of sex trafficking as voiceless. Survivors at a 2018 conference made it clear—they have voices. They have been speaking. It's time for society to see them as humans with something important to say and to listen.[19]

Action 3: Identify Cellphone and Internet Apps

"There's an app for that." The same way there are cellphone applications for getting directions to the nearest restaurant or gas station, playing music you like, and checking your vital signs, there are apps for locating the nearest adult entertainment (which sometimes involves children), holding anonymous secret conversations, and checking another person's location. The same technology that can be used for good can be used for "no good," including child pornography and human trafficking.

In February 2018, two teenage girls showed up at a California airport with expensive, first-class tickets to fly cross country but without identification, appropriate luggage, or their parents' knowledge. They had met a man called "Drey" through Instagram who promised them lucrative modeling jobs in New York. The airline employee who met the girls trusted her intuition that something was wrong and called the sheriff. Odds are good that she kept the girls from becoming victims of human trafficking.[20]

Less fortunate were two girls from Pennsylvania who were trafficked in New York; the man met one teen on

Facebook, sold both through backpage.com, and shared their nude photos through Instagram.[21, 22] To help protect your kids from online predators, take the following steps.

- Familiarize yourself with social media applications and their features.

- Establish ground rules for your child's/student's use of computer and phone.

- Monitor their cellphone use.

- Observe your child.

- Take the time to sit with your child as they work on the computer.

Familiarize Yourself with Social Media Apps and Their Features

Do you know what phone or social media apps your kids are using? Take the following quiz.[23] Can you identify the icons for the following popular cellphone apps and logos for websites and games? Do you know how they can be used?

1.

2.

3.

4.

5.

6.

7.

Answers

1. Snapchat: Can be used for innocent photos or for "sexting." While photos vanish quickly, screenshots can save images that can be used for porn or as blackmail.

2. Facebook: Users must be at least thirteen years old. It isn't kids' top choice for communicating, but Facebook can still hold information about recruiting and selling girls (as Carol witnessed and reported in Fall 2017). Facebook can be linked to many other applications and websites.

3. Whisper: For anonymous confessions. Kids may use it to share fears and vulnerabilities. Sympathetic friends or anonymous predators can invite them to private message sessions. Traffickers/pimps may respond to their fears and exploit them by grooming or building false relationships that look like friendship and love but end with harm.

4. What's App: Can be used to make local or international calls, which is not inherently bad. The reality is that parents can't be with kids every moment to know who they're calling and what they're talking about.

5. Kik: Messages and photos disappear, and senders can't be traced by a regular phone user. As with other apps, kids can submit information that makes them seem older than the required age of thirteen to get an account. It is all too easy for a predator to exploit information your child has shared or to threaten them without you knowing what is happening.

6. Tik Tok (formerly Musical.ly): Kids can use it to create and watch videos with music that can stay local or go viral and that can include videos with adult content. Without parental controls and with kids who figure out how to get past filters, the app can be scarier than it might seem at first glance.

7. Roblox: The wildly popular 3-D interactive game for making friends and role-playing can also be used for predators to target children and for kids to experiment with virtual sex by use of avatars.[24]

Become aware of applications including Instagram, Tumblr, Yellow, Tinder, Twitter, Omegle, Houseparty...the list goes on. Between the time Carol and Ann Marie wrote this paragraph and the time you read it, there will be newer apps and games that are even more enticing to young people around you. Even if you can't keep up with all of them, stay updated as much as possible.

For more information, visit netsmartz.org.

Establish Ground Rules for Your Child's/ Student's Use of Computer and Phone

Decide when—not necessarily based on age but maturity level and need—they may have their own phone and computer, what they are allowed to do with it, when and where they may use it, what to do if someone cyberbullies them or sends them or asks for nude photos, and the consequences for using technology irresponsibly. You can ask for your child's input on decisions, but remember that you are the one with the adult's perspective and should make the ultimate decision. Educate them as you're setting rules. Let them know the following:

- The same apps that can be used to share photos of the family cat can be used for sexting. Teach them what's appropriate to share and what isn't. Be specific.

- Information that might seem trivial or harmless can be used against them. Telling a stranger their location or what they see outside their front door can be put together with other details to find them.

- Information they send can be forwarded. Their communication may not be as private or anonymous as they think. The people on the other end may not be who or what everyone else believes.

Although many parents allow their eleven-year-old children to own a cellphone, Ann Marie decided it wasn't in her eleven-year-old twins' best interests. She had seen what happened when a phone wasn't maintained and monitored. "It's too easy for children to be lured by people who are lying and too easily for children to be manipulated into believing they're texting with another child instead of with a thirty-five-year-old man who is leading them into his arms," she said.

The twins are allowed to use the computer to do homework and play games when they are in the same room as Ann Marie but not in their room or alone. "I understand the need for privacy, but too much privacy at the wrong time can lead them out the door."

Choose a Method of Monitoring
Their Phone Use

Do you know what your child is buying online or from their phone? You would not be the first parent to discover that your child, who is not old enough to drive, bought marijuana, had it delivered to your home, and stashed it in a hiding place before you got home from work. You would not be the first to learn that your child owns a home DIY tattoo kit purchased online or has visited a popular porn site.

Decide whether buying monitoring technology, restricting applications, looking at their phone, or a combination is best for your family.

A county prosecutor says he allows his fourteen-year-old daughter to engage in social media under the following conditions:

1.   He puts the same applications on his phone that she puts on hers, and he becomes friends or connects to her on each of those apps or accounts.

2.   He acknowledges he can't possibly police her phone interactions 24-7, so he makes it clear that he might do a spot check of her phone at any point.[25]

Observe Your Child

Every now and then, watch your child's face as they talk,

text, or connect online or by phone. If you see a child reacting unusually to a message, intervene. Ask what is happening, ask to see the phone, and don't be afraid to report suspicious messages.

Join Them as They Sit at the Computer

Recognize that computers, increasingly complex phones, and social media are not going away. In fact, technology will continue to expand and adapt. Until more adults become involved with children's safety online and society makes some changes, the negative side of humans will reveal itself through technology. To protect your child and begin to change society, you must make the time to watch and work with your child while using any "new" devices.

Carol's friend, Tamara,* doesn't allow her twelve-year-old daughter, Lilly,* to have a personal cellphone but lets her use certain websites on the family's computer. One night after Lilly first got her period, Tamara sat with her at the computer while Lilly searched Pinterest—an application for finding ideas and products—for a tiny hygiene kit to take to school. Inappropriate cartoon-like pop-ups, including one about anal sex, appeared on the screen. Had Tamara not been there to talk to her daughter about what they had seen (and to change Pinterest's default settings to block pop-ups), she may not have found out what Lilly had experienced.

There is access to a street corner in every child's pocket—through their cellphone. How, when, and what they do there can be influenced by you.

If you think someone is exploiting a child online, please call 911 and/or report it to the NCMEC (missingkids.org).

Action 4: Take Stock of Your Vices

With ruthless honesty, list your vices, habits, and forms of entertainment. Do you do the following?

- Drink alcohol—has your child seen you and/or your friends tipsy or drunk?

- Overeat?

- Sneak?

- Lie?

- Cheat?

- Gossip?

- Abuse prescription or nonprescription drugs, legal or illegal?

- Verbally or physically abuse other people or your-self? Have your kids seen you in a fist fight? Have they seen you as the victim of an abuser? (If you have been abused, you can find help from your local Domestic Violence Center, Women Against Rape, or other agencies. They often have hotlines or websites and will protect your identity.)

- Buy sex or have an addiction to sex, porn, or gambling?

Are you a master of self-deceit or denial?

Your kids are watching—intently. They will develop attitudes based on your actions instead of your advice to them. They will mimic what you do. To keep history from repeating itself, **get help for yourself.** In addition to addressing the behaviors that are hurting you and your child, get help for the underlying wounds.

Action 5: Clean Out Your Medicine Cabinet

If the image of a mountain in Nepal is what you think of when you hear K2 (also a term for synthetic marijuana), this chapter will help. It is not a comprehensive discussion of drugs, but it will help you understand the link between sex trafficking and drugs and provide one simple preventative measure: clean out your medicine cabinet.

Carol and Ann Marie have met more women than they can count who numbed (or still numb) the pain of abuse, loss, and physical or emotional trauma through legal or illegal medications. Their addiction or desire to feel happy, high, or without pain was exploited by people who knew what they were doing.

Ann Marie's experience epitomizes a common cycle that links drugs and CSE whether the drugs or exploitation came first. To numb the anguish of childhood sexual and psychological trauma, she turned to crack cocaine. A pimp coerced her into selling sex, and when she didn't follow his orders, he beat her or withheld drugs, causing her illness, anxiety, and fear. To numb the pain of beatings, she used more drugs. To get more, she once gave an IOU to a dealer for about ten dollars' worth of drugs. When she couldn't pay off the IOU because her pimp had taken all her money, the drug dealer punched her and raised the amount she owed. When she ran into a hospital after the assault, he followed her and—in the hospital bathroom—forced a sex act, adding more trauma to her life and reinforcing the need for help in blocking all the horror.

There are numerous drugs used by women who are sold for sex—prescriptions used legally or illegally and under brand names or generic, over-the-counter, illegal street drugs, and more: cocaine, heroin and crack cocaine (and the two mixed), Vicodin, Percocet, PCP, methamphetamine, opioids, and on and on. All can be dangerous. "Drugs and commercial sexual exploitation go hand in hand," said Ann Marie.

Some courts are finally recognizing that sex with a person who is drunk and cannot make lucid decisions is rape, and sexually exploiting a person through her addiction and while she is addicted is sex trafficking. At the same time that this legal recourse can be a small relief, it is better to do everything in our power to prevent the problem in the first place. A simple first step is to clean out your medicine cabinet and help Grandma clean out hers.

Get rid of all outdated prescription or over-the-counter drugs. Dispose of them safely at a community give-back/safe disposal day. If you don't know when or where the next one is happening, ask your local elected official's office.

If you keep a "secret" stash of unused medications in your closet, under your bed, at the back of a drawer, behind other items, or anywhere else, get rid of them too. Face reality: you are the only one who thinks your stash is secret.

If you currently need medications that are opioids or have street value, put a lock on your medicine cabinet.

Also Good to Know: To find out who your local elected official is and get information about related laws, local rehabilitation programs, and safe drug-disposal days, go to whoismyrepresentative.com. Enter your ZIP Code to get names and contact information.

Action 6: Just Say No to Porn

Consider the following:

- At about the same age that girls are first commercially sexually exploited, boys are first exposed to internet pornography.[26]

- Sadly, through porn, young boys are given the impression that sex is commonly abusive, violent, and objectifying and that that's okay. How do they act out the images and concepts they've seen when most of their young female friends want nothing to do with violence and instead are seeking a relationship? They find females who are vulnerable, controlled by someone else, or paid for.[27] In the words of Melissa Farley, author of *Renting an Organ*, "Pornography is men's rehearsal for prostitution."[28]

- Pornography and human trafficking are linked, say researchers. "According to the nonprofit Fight the New Drug (FTND), which relies on dozens of studies for its pornography data, men who go to prostitutes are twice as likely to have watched a porn film in the last year compared to the general population. FTND's research also found that 'when these customers show up, many come ready with porn images in hand to show the women they're exploiting—many of which are human trafficking victims controlled by pimps—what they'll be forced to do.'"[29]

- 49 percent of women "said that porn had been made of them while they were in prostitution, and 47 percent said they had been harmed by men who had either forced or tried to force their victims to do things the men had seen in porn," according to a 2007 study.[30]

The research rings true in Ann Marie's experience. "Quite a few girls got paid in cash, drugs, or a shower to be photographed for pornography for others' use," she said. "One man drove me a very long distance from the city to the faraway suburbs to take naked photos for his own use. Many brought porn or ideas from porn to act out. I didn't like watching it, but plenty of times men insisted on it while they were with me, because it did something for them. A lot of it was freakish, and they wanted me to do the same freakish things to them."

Clear your home of print and internet porn. While traveling, stay at hotels that do not offer pornography channels.

Talk to your kids, and spread the word beyond your family that it's not okay to buy sex. Child pornography is against the law. Porn isn't healthy and can destroy relationships.

Also Good to Know: Signs that your child is seeing or seeking porn: https://protectyoungminds.org/2017/11/02/7-signs-child-viewing-porn.

If you're feeling confused over what porn is like today as compared to a decade or so ago or over conversations about porn and First Amendment rights (freedom of speech), watch the TEDx video, "Growing Up in a Pornified Culture" by Gail Dines (https://www.youtube.com/watch?v=_YpHNImNsx8).

Action 7: Find a New Dictionary

Visit urbandictionary.com. Look at the box of trending words and expressions near the top of the page. What percentage did you know? What percentage were sexual in nature? What percentage would you want your child to use, see, or hear?

It's tough to fight what you don't know exists. If you want to counteract values you believe are negative for children, you need to know some of the slang terms that are commonly used on social media or that they are hearing. Some words might be used while you're in earshot—they just don't mean what you think they mean. Others might not make sense to you.

- Learn slang terms.

- Find out what terms or acronyms they're texting or communicating when you check your child's phone (see Action 3). Some including *fgirl* (look it up on Urbandictionary if you don't know what it means) might pass through parental controls because they've been shortened but don't belong in a child's vocabulary.

- Listen to kids' word choices as you drive your child and others to activities or chaperone a school or faith-based or sports group.

- Look up what you don't know.

- Using reflective listening (review Action 2), ask your child what they think about certain terms. If you have concerns, let them know. Don't be afraid to say that while some language is acceptable in other families (or in classrooms), it's not in yours.

Action 8: Be the Safety Net

Remember that if something terrible happens, you are wired as a parent or other caring adult to help kids out of that situation and to love them. Youth make mistakes, and so do adults. When multiple mistakes are made, the consequences can be catastrophic for the short term if not for the long term. While some stories have tragic endings because of mistakes on the part of children or grownups, strong and caring adults can help turn tragedy into a story with a better ending.

Survivor-leader Rebecca Bender said she left home as a teen because she became pregnant and believed that her parents would not accept her. The man who befriended her and said he'd take her in was a trafficker. He sold her for sex. After the FBI found her and her child during a raid, her parents ensured she had a plane ticket to come home and welcomed both with open arms. Today she speaks worldwide and helps train first responders.[31]

Rebecca isn't the only one. Ann Marie and Carol know too many victims and survivors who ran away because their parents were unsupportive or believed to be unsupportive because a child announced a pregnancy or that they were LGBTQ+. Far too many kids are "thrown away." They are rejected the day they turn eighteen or before they are ready to be launched because they are "too much trouble," won't comply with family wishes, or don't fit in with a parent's new love interest.

- Before you consider giving up on your child or sending them away, weigh the consequences of them being trafficked for sex.

- When things are really tough with your child, know that sometimes muddling through is good enough.

- If you can't accept them or something they do to the point that you are asking them to leave, find a friend, relative, detox center, psychologist, school guidance counselor, homeless shelter, or faith leader who will step in. Action 10 teaches you how to create this sort of friend (a beacon) while your child is young.

In most families, there are challenges that don't reach the level of questioning rejection but feel impossible and relentless in the moment. It might feel like further irritation to hear someone tell you that it won't last forever. Tips to get you through include the following:

1. When a child is heading toward trouble, calculate the risks of that particular mistake. If the risks will be serious, try to coax them down a different path where consequences are less severe. Let them learn by making a mistake that isn't going to damage them permanently but will help them figure out how to confront a mess and change the situation.

    When Carol's first daughter was born, she asked her father what he would have done if she had made any terrible mistakes. "It's okay to let kids make mistakes," he said. "In fact, they need to learn how deal with failure and correct mistakes, but I always made sure that I was the safety net so that mistakes weren't irreparable."

    That philosophy started early and continued for a long time. Family legend holds that when Carol was two years old, she threw a temper tantrum because she wanted to walk down a mountainside without holding anyone's hand. Her parents looked at each other, considered how soft the dirt was, positioned themselves not so far in front of her, and let go of her hand. Within steps, Carol had fallen. She was covered in dirt, tears, and an indignant attitude, but she was unhurt and learned that independence has its ups and downs. Years later, her father used the handy fire extinguisher to quell the flames of a cooking experiment and drove to get her when the clutch of the car ended up on the floor during driving practice.

2. Learn to pat yourself on the back for making it through the hour, or the day, with everyone

alive. Stormy feelings might be rampant, chores may be undone, and life may feel like a complete disaster. Breathe. Sleep. Realize that as long as you're all still alive—even in horrendous shape—tomorrow will be a new day to figure out how to make the situation better.

3. If the unspeakable happens to your child, remember that you can still be there to help them pick up the pieces. You get another chance to become a safety net.

"We are more than our stories," said Autumn Burris, survivor.[32] People who were once victims go on to become consultants, business owners, peer counselors, and law enforcement officers, to have their criminal records expunged, to reunite with their families, and to become brilliant and effective community leaders.

Make sure you take good photos of your child's face on a regular basis in casual and "dressy" clothing. We hope you use the pictures only to have good memories, but if you need them to report your child missing, they are invaluable to help police, the NCMEC, and others look for them.

Today and each day moving forward, hug your child. Say "I love you." Tell them they will make mistakes and so will you. Reassure them that correcting them will be hard, but you are committed to go through it together. If you don't, someone else will, and that someone might be the predator who has no intention of keeping a commitment.

Part 3

PLAYBOOK

What You Can Do: Strengthen Children

ALL PARENTS, CAREGIVERS, COACHES, TEACHERS, AND community members can take the lead in helping kids become stronger and more confident and resilient. It's not enough to protect only your own, because while another child is at risk for harm or being exploited, there is danger that can hurt your child also.

Action 9: Help Them Achieve Their Dreams

In the next ten seconds, write the answer to the following question.

What is your child's (grandchild's, student's, niece's, or other) biggest dream?

If you couldn't answer the question quickly, listen to your child, and learn more. Regardless of how quickly you responded, ask your child what their biggest dream is.

Don't worry if the answer you wrote doesn't match your child's response. On any given day, a new dream or aspiration might be forefront in their mind, or they might not want a deep discussion at the moment you ask. Some kids might not be fully in touch with their greatest desires. The important thing is to start paying regular attention to your kids' dreams and to help them work toward achieving those goals in healthy, positive ways instead of dismissing them or handing them a ready-made solution.

Children's dreams run the gamut—some realistic and some fanciful—from owning the newest technology toy or discovering a cure for a disease that has touched someone they love to sprouting wings and flying. Sometimes helping them work toward a tangible dream is a straightforward path: teaching them to budget and helping them find after-school tasks that they can be paid for in order to buy a bike, guitar, or game. Others will require joining their fantasy world to enjoy the places imagination can take the two of you.

Sometimes dreams are long term, complex, or tied to facing a loss, fear, or void—the way Ann Marie dreamed of a "white picket fence" home and family to fill the lack of love she experienced. Since these may be harder for a child to voice, spend more time with them and observe.

1. Together, watch their favorite television programs, and observe their reactions. What plots resonate with them, and what characters do they identify with?

2. Observe their facial expressions while they are texting or talking on the phone. Whose communication leaves them happy? Whose communication leaves them secretive?

Some dreams are tougher to achieve and take time such as building friendships in a new school or town, after growing out of an earlier childhood friend group, or losing someone special. Talk about ways to become involved with other kids or healthy ways to pass the time while friendships are developing. For Carol, after moving to a new town, a new pet gave her a special friendship and unconditional love while also serving as a draw for other neighborhood kids. Who can resist meeting a baby animal?

Some dreams are unattainable or out of anyone's control—wishing that a parent was back in the picture, that a loved one was healthy and not in the hospital, or that history could be rewritten. Acknowledge that things don't always work the way we want. Find out what is at the core of what your child wants, and help them achieve the same feeling in a way that is positive and possible.

The book *Conversations Worth Having* includes the story of coauthor Jackie Stavros and her teen daughter coping with their husband and father, respectively, who was in the hospital with cancer. Jackie asked her daughter what she missed most and listened intently. Learning that her daughter missed watching the sunset with her dad and the feelings of love that came from that ritual, Jackie suggested that father and daughter watch the sunset from different locations—hospital and home—at the same time to know that each was watching and thinking about the other. Jackie also began to watch the sunset with her daughter at home. While the new situations were not the same as the old, the similar elements and feelings of being loved helped fill the void.

Action 10: Designate a Beacon

Accept the fact that you cannot be everything—the perfect parent, friend, confidante, protector, teacher—at all times to your children.

Kids know by instinct that it is their job to learn to live without you, so they begin practicing independence from the get-go. At two years old, they become proficient at saying no. By fifteen, on an hourly basis, they test their abilities to make decisions and take action without your input.

Even if they ignore or push away your decisions, they need adult teaching, protection, and attentive care. Together with your child, choose a friendly adult presence to act as your proxy listener and beacon. They will be the designated go-to person for conversations when your child is embarrassed or scared to talk to you or believes that you do not have the experience to understand—whether or not you do.

1. With the input of your child (if you have more than one child, you might need more than one beacon), **choose an adult who already knows you and your child and shares your values**. The designated beacon might be a favorite auntie or a close family friend. Listen intently to your child's preferences.

    Do not choose a person who has any agenda for this relationship other than the welfare of you and your child. Never choose an adult who simply has power or a position in the community, church, or school regardless of how moral or sparkling their personality seems. Eliminate someone who you don't know extremely well and who does not know your family's flaws, strengths, dynamics, and quirks.

In a recent case near Carol's and Ann Marie's homes, a prominent and well-respected man was arrested for child sexual abuse and possessing and distributing child pornography. Community members were clueless that for years the father, husband, former serviceman, leader in his church, and township commissioner allegedly had been spreading images of infants and toddlers being abused by adults. As reporters pointed out, people were shocked, because he was well-liked and easy to get along with: "There weren't many people who had anything bad to say about him."[33]

The bottom line is to choose the adult who causes your child's face to light up when they are together. There must already be rapport between the two.

2. **Hold separate conversations with your child and the adult.** Ask your child if the adult is someone they trust—if they would be comfortable talking to or being with the person if you weren't there. Ask the adult if they are willing to serve in this capacity. Be explicit about your values, the conditions of how conversations with

your child will be kept in confidence, and what information will be shared.

3. If you, your child, and the adult concur that this relationship would be beneficial, **hold a conversation among the three of you** and the child's other parent (if there is a strong positive involvement in your child's life). So that everyone hears the same messages, discuss the role of the relationship. Speak honestly, openly, and specifically. **Develop a checklist of guidelines for the relationship by considering the following questions and issues:**

   a. What discussions will be held in confidence? What subjects or information will be reported back to the parent? When will the beacon encourage the child to discuss a matter with you?

   b. What subjects are okay for the beacon to provide advice? Sex? Porn? Gender identity? Drugs? Alcohol? Bullying? Money/allowance provided by the parent? Disclosure of an eating disorder? Cutting or self-harm? Fear of another adult? Harm that is happening to the child's friend and that is worrying your child? Trouble in school or poor grades on homework? Desire for shoes/clothes/phone that "everyone" at school has?

   c. Under what conditions must another conversation take place between the child, beacon, and you, or should the rules for the relationship be overridden? When the child's safety is at risk? When there is the need for a medical opinion or treatment? At certain ages or as the child's level of maturity increases?

d. When can the beacon take action on behalf of the parent? When picking up the child after school or an activity? When the child asks to be picked up from a party where there is alcohol, drugs, or abuse? May the beacon and child go shopping or to a sporting event or pizza place together?

4. **Check in** every now and then privately with both child and beacon to find out how the relationship is working.

You will need to face issues and questions along the way. Are there secrets from your past that your beacon knows and that you have not faced or told your children? Some secrets and information are appropriate not to share or should be shared only at certain ages. Other secrets are not as secret as you think. You may not want your children to confront you with the news that the hairdresser let it slip that the woman your children call their grandmother isn't related to your family. You might feel awkward about not disclosing earlier that you adopted your child when, as an adult, he says that he figured it out in a high school genetics class.

Remember that as a parent or guardian, you have final responsibility for the welfare of your child. Others have a moral obligation (and teachers, ministers, therapists, social workers and mandated reporters have specific legal obligations) to a child who is living with trauma including reporting an abusive parent. Ultimately, a designated beacon can provide one more point of protection for your child.

Case in Point

Carol, her husband, and their daughters chose family friend Annalie as the daughters' beacon when they were in middle and high school. Annalie was ten years younger than Carol and more gregarious, and she had been more rebellious when younger. She was smart and cool. Carol's family loved her sense of humor, candid way of speaking, and willingness to confront situations other people didn't want to face. Carol's family and Annalie's family were close friends and shared many values.

Unless there was a medical or safety issue that had to be reported to the parents, the entire family gave Annalie the discretion to disclose the conversation or not. She became known as the beloved "shoe fairy" who would take the girls shopping for shoes when they couldn't figure out how to fix a simple bad day. She was a true friend when crises occurred. Now an adult, Carol's younger daughter serves as a beacon for Annalie's kids.

Action 11: Develop Code Language

Develop a unique code—a method of speaking or set of words—with your child that you can use to combat peer or adult pressure while in the presence of those peers or adults.

Coauthor Carol moved to a new town when she was eleven years old. Having to make new friends at an unfamiliar middle school when she was awkward, shy, and of an age group that is particularly vulnerable to female peer pressure was difficult. Breaking into established cliques and groups was rough.

When Ally,* the girl across the street, invited her to join activities that made Carol uncomfortable, she hated to say no. Common to preteen girls, she was afraid that a no would cause her to remain friendless, isolated, or be teased because she didn't appear "cool." In a rare moment of revelation, Carol confided to her mother that the neighbor girl sometimes wanted her to do things she didn't want to do—nothing terrible or harmful but not her style. Carol said she felt put on the spot when Ally accompanied Carol to ask her mom, often doing the negotiating, smiling and working hard to persuade Carol's mom to give permission.

Carol's mother listened intently to her daughter's feelings of loneliness and acknowledged the difficulties of trying to belong in a new place. There was no hint of cajoling Carol into joining unwanted activities to become more popular in a new school. Instead, she helped Carol build her own moral compass while having faith that kids with compatible interests and values would be drawn to each other eventually.

Carol and her mom worked out a system of communication to decline invitations until Carol became strong enough to shrug off peer pressure and develop a voice. If Carol said, "Ally wants me to go to the movies with her," no amount of pleading, cajoling, or drama by Carol or Ally would change the kind but firm response of no. There were no lies—no false excuses that they'd be out of town or fabrications that could cause later problems. If Carol said, "I'd like to go to the movies," her mother would say yes if all else was fine.

When they used the code language and Carol's mother said no, Carol, Ally, and others were part of an interaction that had a truthful response modeled by a centered adult. At the same time, Carol was not labeled a "party pooper" by her peers even when she wasn't part of the party. The code language worked well; Carol made friendships that were healthy for her, and over time, she learned to trust her voice and instinct.

Work with your child to adapt Carol and her mother's code language or develop one of your own. Use it to combat peer pressure or to send a signal that an influential adult wants a child to engage in an activity that they don't want to do. For example, even when a sports coach or art teacher has the best intentions, a child may not want to attend extra practices or perform at certain times. Using role-play, practice a couple of conversations so you both know how to do it and recognize the code language when it's needed in real life.

Similarly, **develop safety words** to be used when someone else needs to pick up your child from an activity and **you can't be there or get word to your child about a change in schedule.** Let your children choose words they will recognize. Share the safety words with another adult only when needed. After the code is used once, change the safety words the way you would change a computer password that may have been compromised.

"To an uniformed and impressionable child, it appears as though being a pimp is the way to get beautiful women and to be seen as 'cool' in the eyes of the culture," a college student wrote in a blog.[34] She pointed to pop culture and music as a star-studded vehicle that delivered exciting messages glorifying "pimpin'"—sex trafficking—and influenced millions of kids worldwide.

The lyrics of super-celebrities Jay-Z and Kanye West are examples: "You know how many hot bitches I own?" As of 2017, a YouTube video of a performance with that song line was viewed nearly 185 million times.

Similarly, Eric Tankel, a former heroin addict and now a rehab counselor and antidrug activist, talks about the influence of popular music and images on his path to addiction. When he found prescription Vicodin pills in his home, he was curious about them because he recognized them as the pill depicted on a CD cover by best-selling rapper Eminem.[35]

The next time you're in the car with your children, **ask to listen to their music**. Ask to listen to the tunes on their phone or to find the radio station with the music they like (note the station so you can listen again later with or without them). Ask what they like about the music style and a particular song. If they need a prompt, ask if they like its creativity, beat, energy, the story behind the lyrics, or the band. Ask if the music expresses how they feel and what that feeling is.

Afterward, once a week when your kids are not in the car with you, listen with an open mind and ears to the music they are listening to. The more you are willing to learn and the more you know about their favorites, they more you will build common ground for conversation. Find out what lyrics they might be taking to heart and what images are associated with the band. If you don't understand the lyrics, do a Google search on the song and slang and then ask your kids about them. Determine whether there are values and concepts in the songs that concern you and if there are ideas in the lyrics that are harmful or that could desensitize them.

Rather than having a kneejerk reaction to some music and banning it, calmly tell your child you've been listening to (name the specific tune and artist). Ask these questions:

- Do they like it? If so, what do they like about it?

- What are they lyrics, and what do they mean?

- What do they think of some of the ideas expressed in it?

- Share your concerns with them, and ask what they think of your concerns. Are your worries founded? Even if they say that the music doesn't influence them, ask if it influences their class-mates or friends. Do other kids they know become desensitized to drugs, degradation of other people, or violent ideas?

On a positive note, you might find that there is some good music out there that you have been missing. On the flip side, you might find that you have an opportunity to help your child see what a mature adult thinks about trends that could have a negative impact.

Action 13: Take a Stand on Fashion

The next time your child comes home, observe their clothing.

1. Make a mental note of their overall outfit (jeans, dress, jacket) and appearance and activities they participated in while wearing the clothing (attending school, hanging out with friends, playing a sport, watching TV at home, etc.). Note the colors, how tight or revealing, how practical for the activity, cleanliness, etc.

2. Before asking them about their choices, visit a few websites including stores where they like to shop and stores that are advertised as serving children their age. Note what's trendy, what you've seen other kids wearing, what fits your family's style, and what strikes you as appropriate or inappropriate.

3. If your child is wearing something that you like, let them know they look good. If your child is wearing something (or wearing clothing in a certain way) that causes you discomfort, ask questions, or ask your designated beacon to ask if you are perceived as too judgmental or don't understand current trends. Take a photo to be deleted after you've discussed it, or ask them to look in the mirror with you. What do they like about the clothes? How does the outfit make them feel? Do they know how others perceive the outfit? Does it make sense for the activity?

Do girls understand the effect revealing clothing will have on schoolmates or older males? Dig deeper into their answers. Do they really understand what the implications are? Ask what they see and think, and point out what you see and think. Moms, ask your daughter to have a similar conversation with her dad if he is supportive and looking out for her well-being.

One of Carol's friends asked a middle school girl at her church about a photo she had posted online. The girl replied that she wanted to look sexy. When the adult asked what she meant by wanting to look sexy and what the photo was saying to other kids, the early-adolescent girl replied in common slang terms that she wasn't providing oral sex, she just wanted to look great. That was the start of a vital conversation.

When parenting or coaching women who are transitioning out of CSE, Ann Marie draws on her experience. "I've seen fourteen-year-old girls who look like they are twenty-five by their hair, clothes, makeup, and actions," she said. "Now when I see someone wearing a shirt that is cut too low or a skirt that is too short, I ask them to look in the mirror and tell me what they see. They'll tell me their breasts are showing and ask what's wrong with it. I point out that I see them too, and it's not appropriate for being outside."

During one conversation with her daughter, Carol came to a new perspective. Expressing her opinion about wearing a shirt with tiny straps to school, her younger daughter listened and then talked about what other students were wearing. The daughter also talked about the no-nonsense attitude she wore each day and that others' provocative attitudes and actions sent a stronger signal than any clothing they wore. Carol not only okayed the shirt but was able to take the opportunity to realize and express admiration for her daughter's values.

Ann Marie and Carol concur. An ultimatum about clothing isn't as effective as listening and making them part of a wise decision.

Other action items include the following:

* Teach your children that clothing advertisements are sending a message about making buyers happy whether or not they are based in truth. The first and foremost goal is to make money for the company, not to ensure a buyer's happiness. Work with kids to consider what the ad suggests will be the result of wearing the clothing, if that goal is desirable, and what will get them what they want.

* Consider any mixed messages you might be sending.

Years ago, a friend and I took our thirteen-year-old daughters to the mall so they could shop for dresses for a school event. My friend's daughter tried on a slinky, black cocktail dress appropriate for a twenty-four-year-old woman. She paraded around in it for a few minutes and began to whine and wheedle to buy the dress. Although there was a hint of scolding in her mother's voice, her eyes shone as she said to me, "She looks great in it, doesn't she?" Realizing that the mother was struggling with issues of her own identity and having a momentary lapse of judgment, I turned to the daughter and said, "Put that one back on the rack, and find a dress in the junior department that will be great for you to wear this week."

- Speak out when manufacturers and retailers show poor judgment. In January 2018, pressure on online retailer Amazon resulted in pulling children's clothing featuring the slogan, "Slavery gets shit done."[36] In 2017, consumers railed when they believed Victoria's Secret was sexualizing young females through a new line of underwear. Like Dr. Tanya Thames Taylor, a college professor who has spoken out against "infant beater" shirts that make light of the term "wife beater" and "pimp and ho" Halloween costumes, say something about clothing that desensitizes society's reaction to violence, trafficking, injustice, and the sexual objectification of females. It can make a difference.

If there are kids in the community who don't have strong parents or advisors, step in to protect them as you would your own child. In a neighboring town, a church holds a pre-prom night for underserved teens. In addition to making beautiful gently worn dresses available, they coach girls on appropriate attire for a high school event and safe dating practices.

Having conversations about clothing and setting boundaries for appropriate attire alone won't stop people from looking at your daughter or others or inoculate them from trafficking, but engaging in the discussions and sending the signal that their well-being is important enough for you to stick your nose in their business and that you care sends a bigger message than you think.

Important note: If you or someone you know has been raped or sexually assaulted, *never* blame the victim or the victim's clothes. The perpetrator is the reason the crime happened.

Action 14: Sex and Love: Get Used to Being Uncomfortable and Talk

Talk with your kids about every subject under the sun, especially the uncomfortable ones. Talk about sex, love, human trafficking, and sex trafficking even if you are red in the face, feeling awkward, and sure that you and your child would prefer to be doing anything else instead of having that conversation.

In language and concept appropriate to their age, talk about sex, what it is, what your family believes, when it is appropriate to have it, its potential consequences physically and psychologically, and the right to say no. Whether or not you believe they are listening or they look like they are engaging, keep going.

When speaking one day to a group of teenage girls who were pregnant or already moms, Carol learned that they believed that once they had removed any clothing, they did not have the right to say no to sex even if there was an act they didn't want to do or if harm was involved. Finding out what they believe is a big step in helping them understand what is legal, moral, and supportive of their well-being.

Regardless of their gender, teach them about consent—"no means no" and "only yes means yes." Let them know it's not okay to buy sex. Address the subject of sex and sex trafficking in a way they can understand. Ann Marie taught her twin daughters about it at an appropriate level by the time they were eleven years old.

It is never too early to talk about love. Teach your children in word and action: Love does not include harm or violence. Love does involve honor and mutual respect.

Loving relationships work for everyone's health, safety, and well-being.

Carol and Ann Marie are often asked what programs are presented in school to educate children about human trafficking. The answer is different in every school district. Some have no education. Some have special programs that deal with it directly or along with related issues: good touch/bad touch for elementary students, sex education during biology, and safe dating (domestic violence) or job preparation (sexual harassment in the workplace) for older students. Ask your school district what it offers.

Sometimes faith-based groups hold programs specifically about sex trafficking for youth and their parents.

There is no substitute for parents or primary caregivers talking to their child one to one and having more than one conversation.

Action 15: Journey Together

Pull out your calendar. Count the number of activities you and your child(ren) did together last month—not the number of activities you just drove them to or the sports events or concerts you only watched them in (although those may have been wonderful morale boosters or may have led to activities together to celebrate a "win" or a conversation about the activity) but the ones during which you both engaged in a common goal or experience. Include working side by side on chores such as preparing meals, gardening, or shopping for household needs.

How many activities or hours of activity did you spend playing or working together? How regular were those interactions? Daily or weekly? During how many of those did your child learn skills or values for later in life, and what were they?

How much time did you spend just "being" together?

Walk with your children through life. Make them partners or part of your team as you keep your household going. Share challenges and dilemmas (not big ones—your child is not your emotional dumping ground), and talk through decision-making processes. These interactions give them problem-solving skills and resiliency they can use this week and later in life. They impart values in a way that is better than simply telling them what to do.

Kids can make better decisions when they've practiced making them in real life with you. Engage them even in elementary school with the following situations:

1. Tell them, "We can afford to do one special thing today, and there are two possibilities. What would be best?" Show how you work out options—budgeting, prioritizing, writing and comparing pros and cons, or whatever way works for your family. If they are beginner readers, use pictures, stars, and happy or frowny faces.

2. Tell them, "It's gorgeous outside, and I'd rather play, but chores need to get done. How can we do both?" Use the situation to introduce time management—without necessarily using that term—and talk about needs versus wants.

Incorporate lessons about money into your daily lives. At a young age, let them hand money to a storekeeper, and later ask them to help compare prices. Teach them about the value of money and work. One survivor who was trafficked from the ages of fourteen to eighteen never had any money and was forced to wear whatever her trafficker gave her. After she was recovered by law enforcement, she received help from a wonderful case worker and acquired her first job. She asked her case worker if $10.50 per hour was a lot; she didn't know whether it was a reasonable amount or not or how to determine if she would be able to cover the cost of food, an apartment, and clothing.

List the television programs and commercials or movies you watched together in the last month. Ask what they thought about the language, sex, use of money, how girls were portrayed, what life looked like for the main characters, and how that differed from yours. Talk about the commercials—what are they telling society to value? Ask your kids how they feel about that. Tell them how you feel.

Know where your children and their friends are on weekends. Call around if they're not home when expected. In a 2015 case of sex trafficking of two Pennsylvania girls, two mothers didn't report their daughters missing for a weekend. A sister and a caring aunt discovered that the girls were being sold in New York.[37]

The sky is the limit on activities to engage your kids. Use everyday occurrences as opportunities to guide them, include them, and prepare them for later experiences.

Action 16: Protect Friends, Not Secrets

Tell your kids "protect friends, not secrets."

After a presentation about sex trafficking for youth and

their parents, a mother and daughter—Marie* and Izzy*—approached Carol. The list of red flags for potential human trafficking, in combination with the story of a teen groomed for being sold, led Izzy to disclose a secret. Her best friend, Emmy,* was sneaking out of the window while her parents slept to date a twenty-eight-year-old man. Emmy and the man sent each other texts and met at his apartment where his guy friends would hang out and party. Izzy thought it was odd but kind of cool and adventurous that Emmy had an older boyfriend, so she had kept the secret until the day of the presentation. Izzy told Marie, and together they talked to Carol and called the police.

See chapter 17 for a more comprehensive list, but take a look below at the signs of trafficking or being at risk for trafficking. Many of these described many students in Izzy's school, and when seen in combination, Izzy became scared that more was going on with Emmy than she thought.

- Many victims suffer from depression.

- Many have low self-esteem.

- 75 percent abuse drugs, and 27 percent have alcohol problems.[38]

- Two-thirds or more have experienced sexual abuse or assault as children.[39]

- Some are teenage girls who appear oversexualized, receive expensive gifts, and are dating an older man.

- They don't know or believe they are being trafficked. They don't believe they have a pimp/trafficker; they call a male a "boyfriend" or "daddy" and have been sold the false promise of romance.

- The average age of formal entry into CSE in the United States is eleven to fourteen years old.[40]

With your child, develop an age-appropriate list of guidelines of what is not okay to keep secret and what is. Agree upon who the child will tell—you as their parent, their designated beacon (see Action 10), a therapist, a teacher/school counselor, 911, or another resource. Be specific. Instead of saying that the child will talk about anything that harms someone, specify who your child will tell if she is pregnant, if a friend is using heroin, or if a classmate is suicidal. Tell your child that it may not be easy to speak up on behalf of someone else, but that's part of being a leader or hero when protecting or helping others.

Be prepared for them not to speak out, and make sure your eyes are open. Be ready for them to divulge information when you least expect it (as you're preparing to go to bed at night is common) and their troubles are deeper than they thought could happen. Be prepared to be astounded and to believe when your child is a leader and risks their peer credibility to help someone who needs it.

Also Good to Do: Watch the short video *Chosen* by Shared Hope International with your teens and other families. View the trailer at https://www.youtube.com/watch?v=7xdkNE8Jp9E. Let it spark conversation, and listen to what they have to say.

Part 4

PLAYBOOK

What You Can Do: Build a Safer Community

Help children by building a stronger, safer community. While there are any traffickers, pimps, pedophiles, pornographers, or johns interested in any kid, they are interested in yours.

Some children and animals don't respond to immunizations. The way to protect them from disease is to keep the rest of the "herd" from contracting the disease and passing it to the member who doesn't have immunity. It is no different with fighting human trafficking. We need to build better communities and environments that aren't conducive to the crime, because parents cannot be with children every moment of the day (nor should they be), and a child who is not vulnerable one day might be vulnerable the next. Get to know and strengthen other peoples' kids, not just the ones you think you like. Get to know and strengthen other parents and people who are influencing kids in your community. Make every neighborhood a place that a sex trafficker doesn't find interesting or ripe for business.

As the title of Julian Sher's book about sex trafficking tells readers, a girl may not be your daughter, but she is *Somebody's Daughter*.

Action 17: Know the Signs and Who to Call

"Once I asked a girl in the park why she had a tattoo of the name of her pimp down her back and buttocks," said Ann Marie. "She said, 'Because he loves me!' Tattoos were part of the life. Most of [the victims] had them."

Many victims of sex trafficking are branded. Often ink designs include barcodes, dollar signs, money bags, or their trafficker/pimp's street name—indicating that they are property—on the neck or lower back. Many brands are done with home kits under illegal conditions, without signed consent forms, under the legal age, and in less-than-sterile conditions.

After being sold or transferred from one pimp to the next and new names or designs added to their skin, women realized that earlier pimps didn't love them. Ann Marie said, "Now they understood they were branded for life."

Tattoos are just one potential indicator of being trafficked, and they may be used to identify a missing victim because they don't change quickly, the way clothing or hair color can.

Adapted from the Department of Homeland Security's "Blue Campaign" plus a few others,[41] indicators of human trafficking include the following:

- Disconnection or isolation from family, friends, and previous community relationships

- Dissociation or disconnection from "themselves"—may look like ADHD, anxiety, or mentally "checking out" or daydreaming

- School absences

- Sudden or dramatic changes in personality or behavior

- Signs of mental or physical abuse including scars just under the hairline, bruises, or cuts

- Substance abuse of drugs or alcohol

- Displaying fear and distrust, especially around authority figures or law enforcement

- Asking for permission or deferring to others for decision making

- Lacking food, sleep, water, and/or medical and dental care

- Owning few personal belongings (may carry a few things in a bag), continually wearing the same clothes

- Not permitted to speak for themselves or seems coached on what to say

- Appearing to be homeless or in an unstable living situation—lack of consistent hygiene and clean clothing

- Loss of freedom of movement or controlled by someone else

- Unprofessional-looking tattoos with dollar signs or a barcode

- Oversexualized teen girl with an older boyfriend and recent fancy gifts, a large amount of cash, or an unexplained hotel key card

Not every victim will have every indicator. Some indicators describe a lot of people who are not necessarily victims of human trafficking, adding to the ambiguity, but as a general guideline, if a youth shows several red flags and your gut instinct tells you that something feels wrong, something is wrong. Since most victims don't identify as victims—they believe they are in love or at fault for being "bad"—they won't ask for help.

If you see something, say something.

> If you see danger or suspect that a child is in danger, call 911. Provide the address of your location, physical description of the potential victim or perpetrator including approximate height and weight or build, sex, color of skin, eyes and hair, any tattoos or identifying marks, and license plate if a vehicle is involved.

If you suspect human trafficking but aren't sure, call the National Human Trafficking Hotline at 1-888-373-7888. You can also silently text the hotline at BeFree (233733). If you suspect a massage parlor is giving more than massages, a hotel hallway has a continual stream of men coming and going at a door at night, a nail salon or another shop seems like a front for other business (curtains or blinds are usually closed, cameras face outward, a back door is used by male clients, and a parking lot in the back of the building is busier during unusual hours), call the hotline. It can be anonymous and confidential. The hotline will alert the appropriate law enforcement and social service agencies in the geographic location where the tip is reported.

If you are on a website or social media site where you see or suspect sex trafficking, call 911 or the hotline, and report what you saw to the website itself.

Never put yourself in harm's way. Let law enforcement do its job.

If you are wrong, no one will criticize you, but if you're right, you might help save a life.

Also Good to Know: During presentations, people ask how they will know it's time to call 911 or the National Human Trafficking Hotline. Carol and several people she has coached to call 911 or the hotline say that their intuition told them in that moment. Your intellect may question whether there are enough red flags, and your emotions might tell you you're making a mountain of a molehill, but trust your gut.

You don't need to investigate. Leave that to expert law enforcement. You do not need to feel guilty if your tip turns out to be nothing. Ann Marie and other survivors say they wish that a nosy neighbor had been more interfering. As a cop said, "I'd rather tell a family I was sorry for bothering them than to tell a family their child is dead."

Action 18: Reframe—Humans, Not Riffraff

What words and images come to mind when you hear the word "prostitute"? Chances are you think of words that are dirty, insulting, or profane. The images are probably dirty or dishonorable.

Call people what they are: humans.

The words we used to describe people shape our emotions and behaviors toward them. If you call a female a filthy name, you will likely physically or mentally distance yourself from her—withholding compassion, speaking disrespectfully to her or about her, and perhaps walking across the street to avoid her. Calling a woman or thinking about her as a body part, animal, or object dehumanizes her and sets her up to be treated as such.

What words and images come to mind when you hear the word "victim"? You may think of someone who is sad and needs help. You are more likely to put yourself in a victim's shoes, think "there but by the grace of God go I," and figure out how to help directly or indirectly.

What do you think of when you hear the word "survivor"? It may spark thoughts of strength, courage, and resilience and instill a willingness to help where or how help is requested.

"We are all humans. We have names," said Ann Marie.

Name-calling has become acceptable public behavior: bad hombres, deplorables, and more. While it's tough to put the proverbial cat back into the bag, let's give it a try.

- Start using the term "victim" instead of "criminal" when you hear about or read about a case of a female's arrest for CSE.

- Erase the terms "child prostitute" and "teen hooker" from your vocabulary. Kids who are paid for are by definition victims of sex trafficking. They have been raped.

- Use the term "commercial sexual exploitation" instead of "prostitution." As discussed in chapter 1, few people choose to have sex ten to fifteen times per day if there is any other option.

* Recognize that, over time, some former victims move past being called "victims." They want to be referred to as "survivors." Some do not even want to carry the burden of being a "survivor" after a while. They want to be known as the person they are today: a consultant, author, baker, counselor, parent, or other role. Some refer to themselves and other women who experienced similar situations as "surthrivers"[42] or "members" because they are members of society.

What you call someone becomes what you think of them. When you hear yourself say the word "friend" or "enemy," it affects your emotions, facial expressions, and body language and eventually your actions toward that person. Over time, you create a relationship based on what you call them.

Whenever you are tempted to refer to someone as riff-raff, reframe them as a human.

Action 19: Educate Your Community

Educate others in your community while you educate yourself. As that happens, you will find people who are similarly interested in working against human trafficking, protecting children, and helping survivors. Work together to help a reputable, antihuman trafficking organization that will further mentor you. Ask survivor-leaders to be part of the process.

What and How to Educate

1. Start by showing the need in your area. Show estimates and common types of human trafficking/modern slavery in your state using National Human Trafficking Hotline statistics (humantraffickinghotline.org/states), country through the Global Slavery Index (globalslaveryindex.org), or the US Department of State annual Trafficking in Persons Report (state.gov/j/tip/rls/tiprpt).

2. Invite a survivor, expert, author, representative from the FBI, Department of Homeland Security or local law enforcement, an antihuman trafficking organization member, local social services staff member, or a combination of presenters to speak at a conference, meeting, or educational presentation. Make sure they have a few years of experience working with the issue. For social service agency representatives, residences for homeless people, domestic violence and rape victim responders, and addiction centers are a good place to start, because their work sometimes overlaps with the issue of human trafficking. Ask Carol and Ann Marie to speak or join a panel discussion.

    Please compensate a survivor for their time and travel. They have worked enough without pay and in a position of exploitation. Let them know their unique expertise is valued and deserves fair compensation.

3. Share this book and others with other parents, guidance counselors and teachers, sports coaches, leaders of Scouts and boys' and girls' clubs, church youth group leaders, elected officials, moms' groups, book clubs, and the local media. Donate a copy to a library, school, or church. Find out if there are libraries, schools, or nonprofit organizations that help kids on a shoestring budget and don't have a budget for resources. Give them your copy when you've finished.

Other valuable books are *Girls Like Us* by Rachel Lloyd, *Facing the Monster* by Carol Hart Metzker, *Paid For* by Rachel Moran, *Somebody's Daughter* by Julian Sher, and *The Slave Next Door* by Kevin Bales.

4. Reach out to civic groups, Rotary, Kiwanis, and Lions Clubs, service and social work sororities, and gender/women's rights organizations to share what you've learned and find out what they are doing. You might be surprised to find out that many are already hard at work on the issue. They might be surprised that you're working on it too.

5. Check out the following resources, and contact nearby professional organizations to refer them to useful websites geared specifically to them:

• For lawyers and elected officials: Villanova Law Institute to Address Commercial Sexual Exploitation provides technical assistance for policy makers and legal responders to victims (csein-stitute.org); Shared Hope's Center for Law & Policy includes grades for state laws and legislative support (sharedhope.org/what-we-do/bring-justice).

- For healthcare professionals: US Department of Human Services' Office on Trafficking in Persons' Resource page offers brochures, assessment cards, and posters in multiple languages to download (acf.hhs.gov/otip/resource-library).

- For business leaders: Businesses Ending Slavery and Trafficking offers businesses training and consulting to engage hotel, massage therapy, and other companies in preventing sex trafficking and purchasing sex (bestalliance.org).

- For truck drivers: Truckers Against Trafficking trains drivers to recognize and report suspected instances of human trafficking (truckersagainst-trafficking.org).

- For airline employees: The Association of Flight Attendants connects employees with training to become Eyes in the Skies (hiddeninplanesight. org). Delta's Get On Board campaign includes employee training, volunteering, and support for the National Human Trafficking Hotline. Airline Ambassadors International helps with training, education, and prevention.

- For hotel employees: ECPAT-USA helps hotels establish corporate policies and training. Check out ECPAT-USA's Tourism Child-Protection Code of Conduct at ecpatusa.org/code.

- For technologists: Lend a hand to Thorn, an organization that has built apps to help identify and track kids who are trafficked or abused (wearethorn.org).

- For artists: Learn more and help your community get involved by hosting a Red Sand Project, the brainchild of artist Molly Gochman. The community art-activism installations can be visually stunning and can spark further cooperative action. Photos and information can be found at redsandproject.org.

- For clergy and faith-based leaders: Ask for guidance from the Daughters of Charity Office of Migrants and Modern Slavery about identifying and responding to victims before someone discloses they are being harmed, sold, or exploited.

- For teens: In addition to student chapters of Free the Slaves and Rotary's Interact/Rotaract groups that work on antihuman trafficking projects, look for other local student groups. A group of teens is selling indestructible soccer balls (yes, indestructible—they don't deflate after being punctured by stones or fence spikes!) to raise money for scholarships for girls in Vietnam who are vulnerable to sex trafficking. Information can be found at RotaryVietnamProject.com.

If your profession isn't listed here, Google it with the keywords "against human trafficking." There are more organizations doing more great work and offering help than can be listed here. If you can't find an antihuman trafficking group that addresses people in your career, please contact Carol Metzker (her contact information is at the end of this book).

6. Encourage friends and coworkers to watch movies beyond *Pretty Woman* and *Taken*. These movies leave viewers with Hollywood notions of CSE—that victims enjoy big money and glamour or are abducted in another country by citizens of a second nation to head out on a yacht to yet another. Watch *I Am Jane Doe, A Path Appears* Episode 1, *Born into Brothels,* or another documentary. Bring the independent documentary *From Liberty to Captivity* to your town (fromlibertytocaptivity.com).

7. Organize a group of social workers, teachers, and parents in your community to screen the ten-minute video made for youth, *I Am Little Red* (iamlittlered.com). Put together a plan to take the movie and supporting materials to students in your community.

8. Tell your local theater about the powerful play, *Project Dawn,* written by Karen Hartman and premiered by People's Light theatre. Encourage them to contact Karen Hartman about producing it. Buy the first-edition script by contacting peopleslight@peopleslight.org or calling the

house manager at (610) 644-3500. Read it to learn more about Philadelphia's diversion court, Project Dawn Court, and the life of survivors. One of the characters is based on Ann Marie.

Get help from a survivor-leader—someone who has first-hand expertise. A few places to start are Rebecca Bender Initiative, GEMS Survivor Leadership Institute, Survivors for Solutions, Breaking Free, Christine Stark, and Ann Marie Jones, coauthor of this book.

Action 20: Raise Your Antenna

Do you know what couch surfing is? A kid who is couch surfing is staying overnight at different homes in succession without necessarily letting anyone know that it's happening.

Couch surfers who are secretly avoiding abuse or interactions with alcoholic parents or are ashamed of being homeless through poverty or family rejection may not reveal their situation to adults or other kids. They might give the illusion they're just enjoying spending a night or two at your house before heading back to theirs. They might be carrying a small duffel or trash bag with one change of clothes, a phone, and some personal items. They might be living out of their school locker. During the summer, they might be using parks or wooded areas as makeshift campgrounds. Other kids might know but keep their secret. Kids who are couch surfing are vulnerable to human trafficking and other harm.

Keep your antenna out for couch surfing, signs of depression, substance abuse, and physical or sexual abuse. Remember that these situations occur in all socioeconomic backgrounds.

- Does a student appear to wear the same outfit each day or every other day? Is their hair clean? Do they smell like they have bathed recently?

- Do they carry their laptop everywhere they go and ask to charge it wherever they are?

- Do they often stick around for dinner and end up spending a night (or two) until you begin to ask questions? Do they have ready-made answers about how their parents have given them permission to stay?

- Are their stories vague or changing? Do you see them communicating with their parents? Do you know or suspect that there is family strife?

- Do they seem to miss a lot of school?

- Do their health conditions go untreated?

There are different actions to take, depending on the age, whether the youth is in school, and whether you know harm has happened or you need to prevent it. In some cases, an eighteen-year-old individual still in high school is, by law, an adult in some aspects but not ready to be on their own. The bottom line is anytime you see a child in danger, please call the police.

Open your eyes and ears. Some students are masters of disguise and experts at protecting secrets so they don't have to go back to a difficult home life or face being put under the care of a legal/social service system. Given some quiet care, they might disclose what is happening to them.

Using your head as well as your heart, open your sofa or guest room. You have the right to state the rules of your household while they stay such as no drugs, violence, bullying, or sex. You have the opportunity to show them how a loving family behaves: helping each other with household chores, looking out for each other's safety and well-being, speaking respectfully, and sticking by each other even when feathers are ruffled.

Open your mouth. If the child is in school, call a guidance counselor, principal, or trusted teacher. For the safety and privacy of the student in question, school staff members cannot give you information about the student, but you can report your concern for the child. You can also report tips to the NCMEC by phone or online.

Social workers from a residential program for homeless youths eighteen to twenty-one years old once said they could count on five fingers the number of parents who showed up at their door looking for their missing sons and daughters over a decade. They don't just see runaways but kids who have been "thrown away"—cast out of the house before they are ready to become self-sufficient. They have single moms whose new boyfriend doesn't want another grown male in the house and families who cannot afford to feed a child so the oldest is forced out to survive alone. They are rejected because of gender identity, and there are kids whose "bad behavior" is handled through "tough love." There are so many young adults who experience sexual exploitation from homelessness that the center does street outreach to kids "in the life" or at risk for being sold for sex.

By opening your eyes, ears, mouth, and guest room, you may be the person who makes the difference between a child who makes it through a homeless period without extra harm and a traumatized child who is found through a street outreach program.

An Example

A family Carol knew helped a troubled young man in a way that was noteworthy. Jim,* a high school senior, was kicked out of his home by his adoptive parents shortly after his eighteenth birthday. Just weeks before graduation, he wanted to quit school and get a job to pay for his cellphone and an apartment; he didn't have the necessary resources. His girlfriend found out and asked her family if they would help, since he had been living out of a small duffel bag and staying overnight at various friends' homes for a few days each week for more than a month.

Jim's girlfriend's mother contacted his guidance counselor, kept track of the places he stayed to ensure he wasn't sleeping on the street, invited him for dinners, and brought in trusted friends in the community to talk with him and her daughter. She contacted local social services and a shelter where Jim eventually went to stay for a while.

When They Don't Look Like Angels

Often children and teens who are most difficult to like or reach out to are the ones who need it the most. They hurt, so they lash out or numb their pain with drugs. Unable to cope, they spend time trying to survive rather than doing homework. Consequently, a typical reaction from other parents is to not allow the "difficult" child near their kids, further isolating a child who is potentially a victim.

Savannah Sanders—a survivor of child sex trafficking by a gang and who is now an author and advocate working to end human trafficking—reminds adults to "envelope kids with love." Never ostracize a child or family for a child who is being sexually abused or assaulted.[43]

Action 21: Advocate for Better Laws

As Americans deal with big issues including gun control, sexual abuse, and equal rights, they are seeing how influential their voice can be when changing laws and voting for government leaders. Many who were intimidated by the process of figuring out who their government representatives are and how to communicate with them have realized that it's not hard. Furthermore, they've realized that wise public officials want to hear what they have to say.

Here's how to advocate for better laws against human trafficking and better treatment of victims and survivors.

1. Find out how your state measures up on laws on selling and buying humans. Go to shared-hope.org/what-we-do/bring-justice/report-cards, and enter your state. Take note of what the report says. To find out how the United States (or another nation) stacks up against other countries, read the country's narrative section in the most recent annual US Department of State's Trafficking in Persons Report (state.gov/j/tip/rls/tiprpt).

2. Look up your elected official and their contact information. On Google or DuckDuckGo, search for "Who is my legislator" along with the name of your state. You will see links to websites where you can find your state senators and representatives and US senators and representatives by typing in your address.

3. Call, write, or email state officials about laws you want (or don't want) and your US legislators about federal laws. Better yet, set up an appointment, and visit your legislator or staff member in your state's capitol or local office (or in Washington, DC or a local office). Be prepared, professional, and polite when asking them to support specific antihuman trafficking bills or to use their influence with other legislators. Know how a legislator stands on an issue and the committees they serve on. If they are opposing a bill you want, ask what concerns them about the bill and what changes would make it acceptable. Tell them what you see or know to be true that leads you to ask for this law. Let them know that you are a constituent and that you appreciate their support of the bill. Leave them with a clear, easy-to-read summary of the bill with its number and name and points in favor of (or against) it.

4. If you don't understand a bill, ask for help. Shared Hope International and antihuman trafficking organizations can help you by connecting you with local groups working toward

better laws and by explaining why certain bills are needed and others are in opposition to abolitionists' way of thinking.

5. Support a bill by asking legislators to bring it to a vote, telling them you'd like them to vote yes, and by attending a rally, advocacy day, or press conference for that bill.

6. To gain more support, email a letter to the editor of your local newspapers/media to explain a bill and why it is important to members of your community.

7. After the bill is passed and signed into law, thank the legislators responsible.

If an action leaves you intimidated, accompany someone who has done it before and watch/listen.

The first time Carol set foot in the Pennsylvania State Capitol Building in Harrisburg (since a third grade school trip) was in 2013 when abolitionists were working on a law to require certain business and transportation hubs to post the National Human Trafficking Hotline number (1-888-373-7888). Ann Marie was in the building, and they learned by watching lawyers and antihuman trafficking advocates who knew the ropes.

Since then, they have spoken at Capitol press conferences, testified at hearings, and had productive conversations with lawmakers. As a survivor, Ann Marie has a special influence on legislation and legislators. With numerous colleagues, friends, abolitionists, and fellow advocates, they've worked toward the passage of a state hotline posting law, a comprehensive antihuman trafficking law, a law that requires schools to recognize and address trauma and adverse childhood experiences that get in the way of children's development, and a "Safe Harbor" law that keeps children from being arrested for prostitution and locked in juvenile detention centers. They've supported the reauthorization of the federal Trafficking Victims Protection Act (TVPA/TVPRA) and advocated for the Stop Enabling Sex Traffickers Act. Their next steps are to support state and federal laws for a "Nordic Model" of justice: arresting those who buy sex and providing services for people who are being sold.

If Carol and Ann Marie can learn to do this, so can you.

Also Good to Know: If it's been a few years (or decades) since you studied the path from a bill to a law in social studies, read an article that explains it simply. Visit scholastic.com and find "How a Bill Becomes a Law."

Another resource: Swedish Police Officer Simon Häggström talks about the Nordic Model of arresting sex buyers (not the women and children who are being sold) and how it has reduced the number of traffickers and pimps, CSE of women, and violence against women (youtube.com/watch?v=o6O4xzzTqSU).

Action 22: Practice Fire Drills

Quick! What would you do if this happened to you? While driving home from a trip, you stop at a truck stop for gas around midnight. You see what looks like a young teen girl knocking on the door of a cab or the driver compartment of an eighteen-wheel truck. She has a three-second conversation with someone on the driver side and gets in. What would you do? Who do you call, and what would you say?

See the next page for the correct response.

If you need a refresher for signs of human trafficking and who to call, refer to chapter 21. If you feel uncertain or the thought of responding in a real situation makes you nervous, you're not alone. The first time Carol reported a suspected case, she was trembling. The seriousness of the situation, wondering if she was right or wrong, and doing something she hadn't done before added to the emotions. That is why she created these "fire drills," adapted from real examples, so that others can learn and practice responding before encountering an actual situation.

Here are some special notes for acting in a live situation.

- If you are a mandated reporter (teachers, clergy, social workers and others who by law must respond with a certain protocol), follow your mandated reporting rules.

- Never put yourself in harm's way. Observe and report; do not attempt to investigate or intervene. Call authorities, and let them handle the situation with their expertise. You do not have to know all the answers about what is happening to be a huge help, and you do not want to end up as an additional victim.

- If you're feeling shaky or uncomfortable after reporting a suspected case, call an empathetic friend, or do something that helps you become centered again.

- If you know the potential child victim, do not notify the parents. Sometimes they are part of the problem and may stand in the way of an investigation by law enforcement.

Answer to Fire Drill 1

If you see a situation in which a child is being harmed or might be at risk for harm, call 911. Report your location including the address, if you know it, and any specifics about where the truck is parked, the truck's license plate and identifiers (any company name or products painted on the side, colors of cab and trailer, etc.), what the girl looked like (approximate age, hair color, build, clothing, glasses, or tattoos if you can see them), anything you can see about the truck driver, and any other details about your observations you can remember.

Do not intervene. Stay at a safe distance.

Also Good to Know: Truckers Against Trafficking partners with the NCMEC to fight sex trafficking of children. Watch their video at truckersagainsttrafficking.org.

In the shopping center of your yoga studio, you notice that a day spa has more cars in the back parking lot on Friday and Saturday nights than it does during the day. You have seen only male customers. Once a man wandered into your evening yoga class and made lewd remarks before leaving to go next door. The spa door often is covered by closed blinds even during days when it seems to be open. What would you do?

Answer to Fire Drill 2

If your instinct tells you something at the spa might be suspicious, call 911 and/or the National Human Trafficking Hotline at 1-888-373-7888 (it's easy to remember it this way: 888-3737-888). If you call both to be thorough, let them know you have informed the other and that you are making sure both local law enforcement and the hotline have been notified.

The challenge with this spa scenario is that there isn't much information, and you haven't seen any potential victims. It doesn't appear that there is any emergency. It's hard to draw conclusions from such ambiguous tidbits.

This scenario is not simple or straightforward. Traffickers and others conducting illegal businesses or actions are trying to keep truth away from the public and law enforcement while continuing to draw customers. Victims aren't always seen, and when they are, they may not present themselves as victims or even believe they are victims.

The situation could be nothing, or based on real cases, it could be a situation of CSE or sex trafficking. Remember that you don't have to have all the answers, and you shouldn't investigate. Call and report. Ask for anonymity if it gives you the strength to speak up. If you are wrong and the situation is not one of sex trafficking, it's okay. If you're right, you might save someone's life.

Another action item is to **add the hotline number to your cellphone directory**.

Also Good to Know: In 2014–2017, one of the top five venues for sex trafficking in the United States was illicit spa/massage businesses. To find statistics on the types of trafficking, venues, and victims in your state, visit human-traffickinghotline.org/states.

Fire Drill 3

At a family gathering, your thirteen-year-old nephew is playing on the computer and asks you to join him. He says, "I think I see something bad." He shows you a Facebook page (or other website) that has a photo of his partially nude schoolmate in a provocative pose. There appears to be an adult in the background of the photo. What would you do? How would you deal with the situation and Facebook and help your nephew?

While the web page is still up, call 911. Report what your nephew has discovered. Answer the call responder's or law enforcement's questions. Ask if you should take a screenshot to provide to law enforcement in case the photo is taken down suddenly. (If you do not know how to take a screenshot, use the camera in your cellphone, or ask your nephew how to take a screenshot.)

Report the page to Facebook or the website. If you do not know how, ask your nephew to help.

You can also call in a tip to the National Human Trafficking Hotline (1-888-3737-888) to let them know that you have called 911 and notified the website but that you're covering all bases.

Thank your nephew for letting you know. Reassure him that he has done the right thing. Let his parent(s)/ guardian(s) know what has happened, and reassure both the child and adults that you have called authorities for help. If your nephew begins to be upset at night or is ruminating a few days later, and your listening skills (or his parents') aren't what he needs, find an expert to help. Many counties have a free crime victims' center hotline or counseling, and sometimes clergy can help.

Never shy away from asking for help for your nephew or yourself. Don't wait until secondary or reflective trauma— indirect harm that happens when a crime is witnessed or read/heard about—affects you. Human trafficking doesn't hurt only the primary victim. People who know the victim and entire communities are hurt by social injustice.

Two More Actions

1. **Practice observation skills** to become a better witness. Tomorrow, after encountering the first person you see outside your home, close your eyes for three seconds and describe them: sex, hair, eye and skin color, hairstyle, height and weight/build, glasses or tattoos, clothing including shoes, and any other notable characteristics. The next time you are stuck in traffic, challenge yourself and your passenger(s) to glance at and memorize the license plate of the cars in front of and next to yours. Who memorized the most correct digits on the plates?

2. **Share these drills** with a group in your community, a faith-based adult education class, Rotary Club, or Parent Teacher Organization.

Action 23: Help Stop the Demand for Paid Sex

"What most punters [johns] prize most highly are the youngest and least experienced girls."[44]

Bob Morrison, founder of Freedom and Restoration of Everyone Enslaved (FREE), said there were four groups involved in slavery:

- Vulnerable people

- Traffickers who exploit vulnerable people

- Consumers who pay traffickers for sex and slave-made goods

- A society that doesn't understand what is happening or that turns a blind eye toward the system

Money is the fuel that keeps the whole thing going. The estimated total annual profit made from forced sexual exploitation is $99 billion not including profits made on pornography of women and children against their will.[45]

Now that you know what is happening, you can help stop this monster.

Spread the word that **it's not okay to buy sex.** Not here. Not in the next city over. Not in another country (called sex tourism).

Talk to Your Sons, Nephews, Brothers, Partner, and Friends

Share the reasons. Throughout this book, Carol and Ann Marie have shone a light on the ways paid-for sex and sex trafficking hurt everyone.

- Violence and disease are inflicted on victims and their unborn babies (yes, men buy sex with pregnant women).

- Buyers rob themselves and their families of beneficial relationships and warmth. Communities are less safe and less healthy.

- Trafficked children—who are devastated psychologically and physically, arrested and put in detention centers, and often deprived of a full, holistic education—are later passed over for employment and mistrusted by the general public. Later, they have challenges to living happy, healthy, self-sufficient lives in mainstream society.

In short, buying sex contributes to ripping up healthy social fabric in the present and stealing an entire community's future.

Encourage your local school's boys' sports teams to be part of programs like Coaching Boys into Men. Boys learn about respect, integrity, nonviolence, and working against bullying and sexual abuse. (Learn more at futureswithout-violence.org/engaging-men/coaching-boys-into-men.)

Challenge norms. What makes both men and women laugh off the tradition of inviting a stripper/woman sold for sex to a bachelor party? Habit. Never questioning what we've laughed about since we were kids. If we thought a victim of human trafficking was coerced or forced to entertain at the party, we probably wouldn't find it acceptable. Stop tolerating the degradation of any female by justifying it as a case of "boys will be boys."

If you suspect someone you know has a pornography addiction, urge them to seek help from a qualified therapist or group. If you don't know where to start in your area, contact addiction.com or call (844) 768-0189. The call is free and confidential.

Let corporations and businesses know to stop aiding the sales process. Think about all the businesses that support selling humans: websites and phone applications that publicize and promote recruitment and sales of human beings, drivers of company-owned vehicles or taxis that transport exploited people to sex buyers, and hotels that turn a blind eye. Encourage them to encourage better work practices and educate employees. If communication through regular channels doesn't seem to have any effect, contact the investor relations department—the part of the organization that works with stockowners. While many companies care enough about humans to do the right thing without pressure, it might take the fear of their stock price tumbling because of public outcry to make others change.

Get your city involved with Cities Empowered Against Sexual Exploitation (CEASE) (ceasenetwork. org). You might find out that your city is already working with the network to deter sex buyers. Ask how you can help. As CEASE says, "To put it simply: No buyers, no business."[46]

Carol once asked Starr, a survivor of sex trafficking, "If there was anything you could say to the men who paid your pimp/trafficker to have sex with you and they would listen, what would that be?" Starr replied, "I'd tell them, 'You didn't know that I was forced, but you exposed me to pregnancy, STDs, and violence when I should have been in school. Instead of having sex with me, you could have made a difference in my life.'"

Also Good to Know: In less than two minutes, the video on the first screen at demandabolition.org tells you what it is about. In another minute and forty seconds, you can see how a human trafficking organization educated potential buyers in Amsterdam's red light district (youtube.com/ watch?v=y-a8dAHDQoo).

If you're willing to spend fifteen minutes, read "Prostitution Policy and Law: What are the Options?" at nordicmodel-now.org/2017/07/04/prostitution-policy-and-law-what-are-the-options. It discusses why decriminalizing prostitution makes a bad problem worse, health issues, and more. Warning: The article doesn't hold back the truth. The list of menu items at a brothel, as well as other facts, are disturbing. Don't think that sex menus are found only in Europe. Some strip clubs in Pennsylvania and elsewhere have them too.

Action 24: Get Involved

Get involved in an antihuman trafficking group or an organization that helps to better your community. Whether it is large or small, grassroots or established, faith-based or civic, if it works to strengthen people and help them belong, builds healthy relationships, and fosters informed communication, the organization can help prevent vulnerabilities that are interesting to traffickers.

These are a few antislavery/antihuman trafficking groups to consider joining:

- Rotarian Action Group Against Slavery, a network of volunteer humanitarians, members, and supporters in sixty-six countries who give their time, financial donations, and expertise to help communities fight human trafficking/modern slavery and help survivors (ragas.online).

- Students Ending Slavery, a program of Free the Slaves with dozens of chapters at college and high school campuses. If there isn't one at your school, start one (freetheslaves.net/take-action/students-ending-slavery).

- Love146, an organization whose volunteer teams help with fundraising, awareness-raising, and prevention (love146.org/action/volunteer-teams).

- End Slavery Now has a directory of anti-slavery organizations. Enter your US Zip Code or city and country to find one near you (endslaverynow.org).

What to Do with Your Abolitionist Group

Host a fundraising walk or dinner that will raise awareness as well as much-needed funds, organize an educational program (see Action 19), or work together on any of the other action items in this book. Pay a survivor to be part of your work.

Lend a hand to other groups that help underserved or vulnerable youth and families in your community. Recognize that if a parent is under duress, kids are at risk for harm. A few examples for volunteering include the following:

- Read to kids or tutor kids or adults. Many communities have volunteer literacy or second language programs and after-school homework advice that would appreciate your help. Never underestimate the value of your local public library to provide books, computers, information, and other resources to community members you may not know need help. Ask how you can lend a hand.

- Lead a Scouting group, boys' or girls' club, or coach youth at your nearby community center. Even if you are not particularly musically inclined, ask your child's chorus director or band director how you might help.

- Volunteer at a nearby prison. The person you help might be someone who has been sold for sex or bought sex in the past. Your support during their process of change and belief that they can create a better future might do just that. If there is a group that helps children of incarcerated parents, ask what you can provide.

- Bolster your local community food bank with donations of pop-top canned goods (please make sure the items haven't expired) or time. The one in Carol's community is an ongoing source of help when survivors need an emergency bag of food, ingredients for learning to cook, and meals during the holidays. Please don't put soaps in the same bags as food. Sometimes shampoo bottles leak, and sometimes soaps are perfumed; both can render food inedible.

- Supply new car seats, diapers, and other items to groups that aid infants and children. No mother should have to engage in what's called "survival sex": trading sex for diapers, a roof, or other necessities for herself or her child.

- Give new, in-the-package underwear and socks to women's shelters. Ask what else they need. If you are giving used clothing (please, no used underwear!), make sure the items are freshly laundered, without stains or rips, and will raise the esteem of the recipients.

Ask what help is needed most! If they need money, do what you can to provide that. No car seats or clothing get distributed, and no showers can be offered if there isn't a safe space with a reliable, expert staff member.

There are benefits to you and your family that you might not have considered. Working around kids in the community, you'll get to see what clothing they're wearing, hear the music they're listening to, and update yourself on the latest slang and phone apps—things that will give you a better perspective of your kids' activities. Seeing the challenges other people face—and how they meet obstacles you might not think you could deal with—can provide you with creative solutions and a sense of deep gratitude for your own fortune and blessings.

No time to join or volunteer? If your goal is to have more family dinners around the table after full workdays, pat yourself on the back. Leverage your involvement by engaging in activities that your child enjoys, or support someone else's project. Antihuman trafficking groups, survivor programs, and other agencies that do specialized work in serious fields are grateful to receive the financial support that makes their efforts possible.

To make a financial donation to the organizations helped by Carol and Ann Marie, send a check to the following addresses:

The Salvation Army's New Day to Stop
Trafficking Program
4050 Conshohocken Avenue
Philadelphia, PA 19131

Dawn's Place
P.O. Box 48253
Philadelphia, PA 19144

We are truly grateful.

Action 25: Let Your Compassion Run Rampant

When the horrors of human trafficking leave you speechless, lend a hand until you've found your voice.

The first time Carol visited The Salvation Army's New Day Women's Drop-in Center, she witnessed the most extraordinary act of selfless compassion she had ever seen. A woman entered the center (a small refuge for victims experiencing CSE or sex trafficking in a Philadelphia neighborhood notorious for selling heroin and sex). She asked for a pair of socks. Although there were other tangible necessities—gently worn shirts and pants, food, deodorant, and Band-Aids—the socks were all gone. Another victim seeking a temporary safe haven reached down and untied her shoelaces. She offered the other woman the socks off her feet. Most likely she was homeless and had nothing but the clothing she wore, yet she offered her socks without hesitation.

Hundreds of women who receive services at the center have nearly nothing—no secure homes with three nutritious meals each day, no supportive family, no daily hot shower, no access to proper healthcare, no money for underwear, shoes, and socks, no respect from society, and no options. They are purchased for sex, controlled by pimps/traffickers or drug dealers, exposed to disease, and subject to brutal violence at any given moment. They know pain, hunger, want, and need. They do not know the feeling of full physical and spiritual freedom.

It appears that some victims know and practice the act of selfless giving beyond measure. Like Ann Marie taking food to a child who was in the same predicament she was—homeless and hungry—let the plight of another human stir your empathy and propel you to share what you have.

Self-indulgence, road rage, name calling, and inadvertently putting ourselves before others because we are rushed or stressed has become rampant. While everything and everyone else goes a little crazy, take a deep breath, and open your heart.

Take inspiration from that victim who offered her socks, and **perform one compassionate action each day for the next two weeks.** Watch for a ripple effect, and experience what it does for your well-being.

The Last Word: Love Your Children

We pray that we work ourselves out of our jobs and, until then, that we receive the strength and support to continue. We hope we don't meet your son or daughter as a victim. If we do, know that we will do what we can to help them as they find their own way back to healthier, happier lives.

If your child's path is filled with pain and destruction, we share your sorrow. Please take heart. As Ann Marie has shown, it is possible to overcome every challenge. She is living evidence that it is possible to become a survivor who is more than her past—a thriving, self-sufficient, successful member of our community who gives of herself to victims and survivors using her firsthand knowledge and experience.

There are others like Ann Marie. Antonia "Neet" Childs started a bakery, Neet's Sweets (neetssweets.com), that uses a portion of proceeds to help less fortunate people including victims of human trafficking (try her red velvet cake pops).[47] Rachel Lloyd and Rachel Moran, founder of GEMS and an international speaker, respectively, authored pivotal books about sex trafficking (read Lloyd's *Girls Like Us* and Moran's *Paid For*). Brendale McAfee is a staff member at Dawn's Place. Rebecca Bender trains law enforcement to respond to victims. Marian Hatcher, senior project manager and human trafficking coordinator at the Cook County (Illinois) Sheriff's Office, was awarded a 2017 President's Lifetime Achievement Award and has, deservedly, received clemency for her felonies.[48] The list goes on.

We don't want what happened to Ann Marie or any other survivors to happen to any kids. If it does, recognize the resilience, creativity, courage, and strength they have that sees them through their travails. Respect that as they work to make difficult changes. Should your child or any other survivor choose to tell their story, know that telling it will undoubtedly cause pain and could re-traumatize them, yet they do it to educate and protect your community. Honor that.

Our wish is that you will join us in working against human trafficking and protecting every child against monstrous crimes and social injustice. In this book, we list numerous ways to become involved and to give to their organizations and others. Please put that list to good use to counter the playbooks, videos, and instructions for keeping our fellow humans in psychological chains.

Our Hope

Not long before they finished this book, on January 2, 2018, Carol and Ann Marie attended the birth of Ann Marie's second granddaughter. While looking into the face of a little girl recovered from slavery in 2004, Carol could not have imagined that she would look into the face of another family's newborn just seconds old. While homeless, Ann Marie could not in her wildest dreams have foreseen a life that would include being with her daughters and grandchildren, much less witnessing one's arrival.

In addition to experiencing the joyous miracle that comes with the birth of a beloved baby, Carol and Ann Marie felt the power of family, friendship, community, transformation, reconciliation, freedom, gratitude, and awe. They felt renewed hope and, as they did years ago, experienced profound love for a child entering the world.

Carol and Ann Marie felt another surge of protectiveness—wanting to make the world a safer, healthier, and more joyous and free place for this tiny girl and for other children.

Let your children and others in your community know that you love them. Tell them. Show them. Truly loving them provides a more effective shield than you might ever imagine.

Notes

Introduction

1. PHD (Pimp Hands Down), https://www.facebook.com/permalink.php?story_fbid=64195800058.

2. "Engaging Survivors of Commercial Sexual Exploitation in the Search for Justice," Second Annual Survivor-Led Symposium, Villanova Law Institute to Address Commercial Sexual Exploitation, April 6, 2018. Comments gathered during an impromptu public discussion following the final workshops.

Chapter 1

3. FBI Status Report, Chris Swecker, Assistant Director, Criminal Investigative Division, Federal Bureau of Investigation, June 17, 2005, https://archives.fbi.gov/archives/news/testimony/exploiting-americans-on-american-soil-domestic-trafficking-exposed.

4. For reports 2012–2017: FBI Operation Cross Country, www.fbi.gov. For reports 2008–2011: Washington Post, Nov. 24, 2015, http://www.washingtonpost.com/news/fact-checker/wp/2015/11/24/loretta-lynchs-false-claim-on-sex-trafficking-arrests/?utm_term=.27b8cbe46264.

5. "The Commercial Sexual Exploitation of Children in

the U.S., Canada and Mexico," Richard J. Estes and Neil Alan Weiner, University of Pennsylvania, Sept. 19, 2001, Revised Feb. 20, 2002, http://www.sp2.upenn.edu/restes/ CSEC_Files/Exec_Sum_020220.pdf.

6. "Young lives for sale: Why more kids are getting into the sex trade—and how the feds are fighting back," B. Fang, *U.S. News & World Report*, in "Know the Facts: Commercial Sexual Exploitation of Children by Chicago Alliance Against Sexual Exploitation."

7. "Profits and Poverty: The Economics of Forced Labour," International Labour Organization, 2014, http://www.ilo. org/wcmsp5/groups/public/---ed_norm/---declaration/ documents/publication/wcms_243391.pdf.

8. National Center for Missing and Exploited Children, http://www.missingkids.com/theissues/trafficking (2019).

9. "One-fifth of homeless youth are victims of human trafficking," J. DiSanto, Penn Today, Apr. 30, 2018, https:// penntoday.upenn.edu/news/one-fifth-homeless-youth-are-victims-human-trafficking.

10. "Labor and Sex Trafficking Among Homeless Youth," Loyola University (2016).

11. Thorn, https://www.thorn.org/child-sexual-exploitation-and-technology (2015).

12. Thorn, https://www.thorn.org/child-sexual-exploitation-and-technology (2015).

13. M. Farley, A. Cotton, J. Lynne, S. Zumbeck, F. Spiwak, M.E. Reyes, D. Alvarez, and U. Sezgin, Prostitution and

Trafficking in 9 Countries: Update on Violence and Post-traumatic Stress Disorder, in "Prostitution, Trafficking, and Traumatic Stress," 44 (M. Farley ed., Haworth 2003).

Chapter 3

14. "40 million in modern slavery and 152 million in child labour around the world," International Labour Organization, Sept. 19, 2017, http://www.ilo.org/global/about-the-ilo/newsroom/news/WCMS_574717/lang--en/index.htm.

Chapter 4

15. Marlene Carson (speech, "Survivor-Led Symposium: Engaging the Survivor Community in Advocacy, Healing, and Criminal Justice," Villanova Institute to Address Commercial Sexual Exploitation, March 8, 2017).

16. Donna Sabella, "The Role of the Nurse in Combatting Human Trafficking," *American Journal of Nursing* 111, No. 2 (2011).

17. Judith L. Herman, *Trauma and Recovery: The Aftermath of Violence* (New York: Basic Books, 1992).

18. "Young lives for sale: Why more kids are getting into the sex trade—and how the feds are fighting back," B. Fang, *U.S. News & World Report*, in "Know the Facts: Commercial Sexual Exploitation of Children by Chicago Alliance Against Sexual Exploitation," https://temeculaca.gov/DocumentCenter/View/177/Know-the-Facts---Commercial-Sexual-Exploitation-of-Children-PDF.

Playbook Action 2

19. "Engaging Survivors of Commercial Sexual Exploitation in the Search for Justice," Second Annual Survivor-Led Symposium, Villanova Law Institute to Address Commercial Sexual Exploitation, April 6, 2018. Comments gathered during an impromptu public discussion following the final workshops.

Playbook Action 3

20. "Sacramento Airline Agent Credited With Stopping Possible Trafficking of 2 Teen Girls," February 18, 2018, http://newyork.cbslocal.com/2018/02/18/sacramento-airline-agent-stops-trafficking.

21. Special agent, Homeland Security Investigations, Child Exploitation and Human trafficking investigations group, (speech, "Protecting Children Against Human Trafficking," Sept. 30, 2017, Newtown Square, PA).

22. "New York Man Charged with Sex Trafficking" (Scranton, PA: US Attorney's Office, Dec. 15, 2015), https://www.justice.gov/usao-mdpa/pr/new-york-man-sentenced-135-months-federal-prison-child-sex-trafficking.

23. Adapted from Vaishali Bhagwat, "Keeping Children Safe Online," Rotary International Conference, Seoul, South Korea, May 31, 2016.

24. "Roblox: What Parents Must Know About This Dangerous Game for Kids," Family Zone Team, February 24, 2017, https://www.familyzone.com/blog/roblox-parents-review.

25. Tom Hogan (speech, Walk Her Home Event, West Chester, PA, Oct. 7, 2017).

Playbook Action 6

26. Sabina, C., Wolak, J., Finkelhor, D., "The Nature and Dynamics of Internet Pornography Exposure on Youth," *Cyberpsychology and Behavior* 11, No. 6 (2008), https://scholars.unh.edu/cgi/viewcontent.cgi?article=1283&context=soc_facpub.

27. "Growing Up in a Pornified Culture," Gail Dines, TEDx Navesink, https://www.youtube.com/watch?v=_YpH-NImNsx8.

28. Melissa Farley, "Renting an Organ for Ten Minutes: What Tricks Tell Us about Prostitution, Pornography, and Trafficking," in *Pornography: Driving the Demand in International Sex Trafficking*, D. E. Guinn and J. DiCaro, eds. (Bloomington, IN: Xlibris, 2007), 145.

29. "Want to Stop Trafficking? Look to America's Porn Addiction," John-Henry Westen, https://www.huffingtonpost.com/johnhenry-westen/want-to-stop-sex-traffick_b_6563338.html.

30. Farley, *Pornography*, 145.

Playbook Action 8

31. Author interview with Rebecca Bender, May 28, 2015, and Rebecca Bender (speech, "General Session on Ending Slavery," Rotary International Convention, Atlanta, GA, June 12, 2017).

32. Autumn Burris (speech, "Survivor-Led Symposium: Engaging the Survivor Community in Advocacy, Healing, and Criminal Justice," Villanova Institute to Address Commercial Sexual Exploitation, March 8, 2017).

Playbook Action 10

33. "Radnor commissioners president Philip Ahr charged in child porn case," Erin McCarthy, http://www.philly.com/philly/news/crime/radnor-township-commissioners-president-phil-ahr-charged-with-child-sexual-abuse-20171011.html.

Playbook Action 12

34. "Pop Culture and How It Perpetuates Human Trafficking," blog post on LGS Global Affairs, Cailin G., Oct. 7, 2012, https://lgsglobalaffairs.wordpress.com/2012/10/07/pop-culture-and-how-it-perpetuates-human-trafficking.

35. Eric Tankel (speech and discussion at Salonistas group meeting, Malvern, PA, May 25, 2017).

Playbook Action 13

36. "Amazon pulls kids clothes bearing 'Slavery gets shit done'," Kieran Guilbert, Thomson Reuters Foundation, Jan. 22, 2018, https://www.reuters.com/article/us-amazon-com-slavery/amazon-pulls-kids-clothes-bearing-slavery-gets-shit-done-slogan-idUSKBN1FB1OW.

Playbook Action 15

37. Special agent, Homeland Security Investigations, Child Exploitation and Human trafficking investigations group (speech, "Protecting Children Against Human Trafficking," Sept. 30, 2017, Newtown Square, PA).

Playbook Action 16

38. M. Farley & H. Barkan, "Prostitution, violence against women and posttraumatic stress disorder," *Women and Health* 27 (1998), 37-49.

39. David Finkelhor and Angela Browne, "The Traumatic Impact of Child Sexual Abuse," *American Journal of Orthopsychiatry* 55(4).

40. Swecker, https://archives.fbi.gov/archives/news/testimony/exploiting-americans-on-american-soil-domestic-trafficking-exposed.

Playbook Action 17

41. Indicators of Human Trafficking—Department of Homeland Security "Blue Campaign," https://www.dhs.gov/blue-campaign/indicators-human-trafficking.

Playbook Action 18

42. Marlene Carson (speech, "Engaging Survivors of Commercial Sexual Exploitation in the Search for Justice," Second Annual Survivor-Led Symposium, Villanova Law Institute to Address Commercial Sexual Exploitation," April 6, 2018).

Playbook Action 20

43. Savannah Sanders (webinar, "Human Trafficking Prevention in Schools and Communities," US Dept. of Health and Human Services Office on Trafficking in Persons, Oct. 24, 2017).

Playbook Action 23

44. "Prostitution Policy and Law: What are the Options?" Nordic Model Now, July 4, 2017, https://nordicmodelnow. org/2017/07/04/prostitution-policy-and-law-what-are-the-options.

45. "Profits and Poverty: The Economics of Forced Labour," International Labour Organization, 2014, http://www.ilo. org/wcmsp5/groups/public/---ed_norm/---declaration/ documents/publication/wcms_243391.pdf.

46. Cities Empowered Against Sexual Exploitation, https:// www.ceasenetwork.org.

The Last Word

47. "More Than a Survivor," Exhibit at Studio No. 7, Atlanta (closed as of June 19, 2019), May 11, 2015.

48. "Trafficking Survivor Now Helps Others," Jacqueline Rachel, Jan. 18, 2018, http://www.salarmychicago.org/ blog/2018/01/trafficking-survivor-now-helps-others.

Acknowledgments

THE NAMES OF THE COAUTHORS MIGHT LIVE ON THIS book's cover, but hundreds if not thousands of people made this book possible. We are grateful for each and every one of them. Friends, colleagues, researchers, Rotarians, community members of Dawn's Place, mentors, and teachers provided information and served as beacons to light our way.

Thank you to the following:

* Survivors who trusted us with their stories or spoke in public so that we might learn and become better teachers to others: Brendale, Tammy, Marlene, Rebecca, Autumn, Peggy, Starr, and many who remain unnamed.

* Many individual Catholic Sisters, Quaker Friends, and faith-based groups held us up including Sister Michelle Loisel, Sister Eileen White, Sister Kate O'Donnell, and Willistown Friends.

* Anti-slavery and antihuman trafficking activists who worked and continue to work side by side with us: members of the Rotarian Action Group Against Slavery, Philadelphia and Chester County

Anti-Human Trafficking coalitions, JusticeRain Inc., Ace of Oxford, Debbie Wright, Peggy Russell, Diane, Carole, and others. We thank Kevin Bales, Peggy Callahan, Ginny Baumann, and Supriya Awasthi for leading as shining stars.

- Friends, colleagues, and influential people in their fields who took the time to read the book, provide feedback, champion our work, or endorse our manuscript: Mark Little, James Bady, Susan Page Tillett, Rita Nieman, Sami Abdel-Salam, Jamie Manirakiza, George Belitsos, Toni Hill, Sister Jean Faustman, Tojo Thatchenkery, Cynthia Haynes Eshleman, and others.

- Our team at Luminare Press.

Our undying gratitude goes to family members—Eric, Elizabeth, Kathryn, Linda, Malisha, Angelina, Zaydah, Vanitti, Evelyn, and Bill—and those who live their lives as family members—Angie, Annalie, and Phoebe—who gave of themselves each day, shared their strength and courage, and brought out the best of us even in troubled times. Your soaring souls and spirits continue to uplift us.

There are others whom we have not mentioned by name, but we are still deeply appreciative of your role in the efforts to write this book and end human trafficking.

About the Authors

CAROL HART METZKER IS AN ALLY FOR SURVIVORS, AN antihuman trafficking activist, educator, frequent speaker, TEDx salon presenter, and author of *Facing the Monster: How One Person Can Fight Child Slavery*. She has volunteered at Dawn's Place—a residential program for female survivors of human trafficking and CSE—for more than eight years, and she consults with The Salvation Army's New Day to Stop Trafficking Program. She is featured in the documentary about human trafficking, *From Liberty to Captivity*. Carol is a recipient of a Rotary International Service Above Self Award and other human rights/humanitarian awards. Her husband and grown daughters are often partners in her work. Contact her at Carol@serveforsuccess.com.

ANN MARIE JONES IS A SURVIVOR OF SEX TRAFFICKING who helps women recover from the life she once endured. She is a peer recovery specialist at Dawn's Place, where she initiated a twelve-step sexual exploitation recovery program. She is a frequent speaker and an advocate for better antihuman trafficking laws. A character in the play "Project Dawn" by Karen Hartman is based on Ann Marie's experience working toward the exoneration of her criminal record. She was the first recipient of a Rotarian Action Group Against Slavery Freedom Award. She is a mother and grandmother.